The Essential Renewal of America's Schools

The Essential Renewal of America's Schools

A Leadership Guide for Democratizing Schools from the Inside Out

Carl Glickman
Ian M. Mette

TEACHERS COLLEGE PRESS
TEACHERS COLLEGE | COLUMBIA UNIVERSITY
NEW YORK AND LONDON

Published by Teachers College Press,® 1234 Amsterdam Avenue, New York, NY 10027

Copyright © 2020 by Carl Glickman and Ian M. Mette

All rights reserved. No part of this publication may be reproduced or transmitted in any form or by any means, electronic or mechanical, including photocopy, or any information storage and retrieval system, without permission from the publisher. For reprint permission and other subsidiary rights requests, please contact Teachers College Press, Rights Dept.: tcpressrights@tc.columbia.edu

Library of Congress Cataloging-in-Publication Data is available at loc.gov

ISBN 978-0-8077-6402-2 (paper)
ISBN 978-0-8077-6403-9 (hardcover)
ISBN 978-0-8077-7863-0 (ebook)

Printed on acid-free paper
Manufactured in the United States of America

Contents

Prologue	ix
Preface	xi
Acknowledgments	xiii

1. Introduction: Recapturing the Essence of Schools — 1
   The Fork in the Road — 1
   Whipping American Public Schools with External Control — 2
   Being Real — 3
   Recapturing the Goal of American Public Schools — 4
   A Reframing of the Work — 6
   Ordinary Good People Doing Extraordinary Good Work — 7

PART I: A RENEWED FRAMEWORK FOR DEMOCRATIZING SCHOOLS FROM THE INSIDE OUT

2. The Promise: Establishing Common Principles of Teaching and Learning — 11
   Schools as Successful Organizations — 12
   Traditions of (Mis)Education — 15
   Existing Conditions as a Forum for Discussion: Types of Schools — 17
   Developing the Promise — 19
   Principles of Learning — 21
   What to Do with the Promise — 23

3. The Pledge: Creating a Commitment to Make Decisions as a Community — 24
   Developing a Decisionmaking Process — 25

Guiding Rules of Decisionmaking	25
Locus of Control	26
Factors Impacting Democracy in Schools	27
The Ideal Governing Rules	29
Navigating Between Ideal and Reality	32
What Type of Governance?	33
Representative, Direct, and Hybrid Governance	34
Why Do This?	35
If Not Us, Then Whom?	37
Focus on Governance	38
A Final Note About Formality and Procedures	38

4. Problem Solving: Community-Based Action Research to Drive Student Learning — 40

The Critical Self-Study Process	41
Raising Community-Based Questions to Drive Action Research	41
Data Sources for Self-Study	42
An American Tendency: Action Without Study	45
Infusion of Information	46
Ways to Gather Information	47
Giving Voice	49

PART II: THE WORK OF SCHOOL RENEWAL

5. Educational Priorities and Organizational Application — 53

Curriculum Development and Implementation	54
Staff Professional Development	56
Instructional Coaching	57
Student Assessment and Outcomes	58
Instructional Resources	59
Implementing New Practices	61
Stages of Concern	62
Blurring of Tasks	63
Departmental and Grade-Level Plans	64

6.	**Becoming an Educative Community**	**66**
	Change and the Shadows of Our Own Caves	66
	Understanding (De)Motivating Factors: Approaches to School Change	67
	Developmental Needs	69
	Sociocultural Differences	71
	Getting Started	73
	The Need to Identify and Act on Inequity	74
7.	**Dealing with Tough Questions of Practice**	**75**
	With Freedom Comes Responsibility	76
	Moral Authority; Not Imposed Formal Authority	79
	Diversification vs. Competition	80
	The Ability of a Principal to Mobilize	82
	Opportunities to Engage the Larger Community	83
	Why Opportunities Are at the Heart of Renewing American Schools	84
	The Continuum of Renewal	86
8.	**Supporting School Renewal: Important Signals from the District**	**88**
	The Politics of a School Board and District Personnel	88
	Opportunities to Empower	89
	An Age-Old Issue: Equality vs. Equity	91
	Democratic Use of Economic Principles	92
	Developing a District Plan for School Renewal	93
	Fade Away or Facilitation?	96
	Issues in Developing District Policies	96
	The Morality of Decentralization	98

PART III: MOVING BEYOND IDEAS AND INTO ACTION

9.	**Dilemmas of Good Schools: Pinpointing and Moving On**	**103**
	The Issue of Time	103
	External Regulations	104
	Voice	106
	Coordinating with Other Schools	108

Dependence on External Authorities	109
Sequence, Emphasis, and the Pace of Educational Change	110
Dysfunctional Behavior	112
Dilemmas and Decisions	114
10. Conclusion: If Not Now, Then When?	**115**
How to Take This Book and Run with It	116
Restructuring Policy	118
A Sobering Appraisal of the Need to Focus	119
Believing	120
Appendix A: Sample Pledge to Democratic Governance	**123**
Appendix B: The Peakview School Pledge	**129**
Appendix C: A Sample of a Process for Decentralizing Authority to Local Schools by a District and State Invitational Policy	**131**
References	**135**
Index	**139**
About the Authors	**145**

Prologue

> Is Democracy Dying?
>
> —Theme issue of *The Atlantic Monthly* (2018)

Much has occurred since *Renewing America's Schools: A Guide for School-Based Action* was first published in 1993. Let me explain why I sought a major reworking of that widely read text. The changed title, *The Essential Renewal of America's Schools: A Leadership Guide for Democratizing Schools from the Inside Out*, will give the reader some inkling about this new book. It is about returning schools to their original purpose of preparing students for the educated citizenry of an improving and expanding democracy. Such a statement can appear to be mushy, sentimental, and vague, but to realize this goal means implementation of critically important classroom and schoolwide practices that promote academic achievement, participation, and application.

As my mother used to tell me, "May you live in interesting times," and for sure this has been an interesting time of confusion, celebration, anger, demoralization, and stand-up fighting. Since 1993, the economy of the 1990s burst with the end of the dot-com bubble. A contested presidential election was decided by the U.S. Supreme Court, and the 9/11 terror attacks led to the longest continual military engagement in our nation's history. Hurricane Katrina highlighted the horrific living conditions of economically distressed American citizens. The first African American president was elected. The Great Recession was the worst economic recession to occur since the 1930s. The opioid epidemic has gripped communities throughout the country. Attention to health issues and the lack of medical attention to those who are uninsured gave momentum to Congress passing the Affordable Care Act, providing health care to millions of uninsured Americans. The Black Lives Matter movement began, forcing the confrontation of issues of police brutality and racial profiling. Multiple domestic terror attacks and mass shootings occurred, causing more political disagreements about gun rights and laws. The #MeToo movement led by women for women forced a reckoning with male control and domination, and White supremacy in all its ugliness was on open display in Charlottesville, Virginia.

The bitter divide continues to be vitriolic and has created a climate of uncivil war between political views. And most recently, the very foundation of our democracy has been tainted by foreign government interference with our democratic process, children being separated from their parents attempting to cross the U.S. border, and the relentless disagreements as to who is and who is not a member of American society.

So, this is why I, Carl Glickman, sought out the much younger Ian M. Mette, a prominent leader, writer, and activist in the field of school-based change, supervision, and instructional leadership, to collaborate with me as equals in significantly revising this book. It is for those who lead formally or informally—educators, parents, and community members—to address this key issue of our time: educating for democracy. It is bold, it is essential, and it can remake our schools into a powerful and rightful engine of a healthy future.

Preface

The purpose of this book, *The Essential Renewal of America's Schools: A Leadership Guide for Democratizing Schools from the Inside Out*, is to provide a framework that takes democratic ideals and turns them into reality. We know that the real work will come from those in the field—the educators who work hard each and every day to provide students and parents with what they need to receive a quality education. That said, this book lays out premises and practices of how schools can be more democratic, moral, and purposeful.

While we acknowledge there are no simple answers to any problem in education, the root of this work is based on one simple ideal: American public schools are intertwined in the communities they serve. Therefore, it is time to stop believing state or federal politicians can fix our school systems and to turn this logic on its head. Instead, our school systems must feed the basic needs that a democracy was founded on. And it starts by allowing schools the autonomy to return their focus to the needs of students, parents, and stakeholders at the local level.

This will require the leadership of experienced veterans as well as that of young idealists. And while it is always easier to think of a better way to do something than it is to implement an idea into action, it is the only hope we have if we are to keep the American public education system public. To say it succinctly: As educators our goal is to help prepare our students to become proactive members of our society, which is best measured by what students can do with their learning beyond the classroom. We accomplish this by using participatory learning practices throughout the school and its community to make connections between what we teach, what students learn, and how students apply their learning to the larger world.

Chapter 1 provides a framework for school systems to use to reconceptualize their moral purpose, how they positively contribute to a democratic society, and how educators at the local level can work collaboratively with community members to create a narrative of school success. In Part I, we detail the three-dimensional framework used to help practitioners turn ideals into reality. Chapter 2 explores the importance of developing a school promise guided by collaborative pedagogical principles about teaching and learning to explore structures that can help address issues in a local context. Chapter 3 explains the second dimension, which consists of developing a pledge for school decisionmaking around group dynamics and is based on the promise. Chapter 4 describes the third dimension, problem solving through action research, where school systems determine a finite amount of data to be collected and used in order to make informed decisions about student learning.

Part II outlines the internal educational work of schools as well as the policy changes that need to occur within districts, and concludes with the paradigm shift to view school renewal as an ongoing process. Chapter 5 describes the educational tasks (peer coaching, staff development, support of student exploration, valuing teaching experimentation, support of teacher inquiry) that schools and instructional leaders have within their control. Chapter 6 examines the internal focus of providing students, community members, and teachers with a greater voice in order to give more confidence to the democratic process. Chapter 7 raises provocative questions about comparing current educational practices with optimal conditions of learning. Chapter 8 describes the critical role, responsibilities, and policies needed of districts, school boards, and teacher associations/unions to clarify, encourage, coordinate, and support school renewal.

In Part III we ask the reader to move beyond ideas and consider how this important work can be applied in action. Chapter 9 anticipates the various dilemmas and competing consequences of profound school change in terms of resistance, miscommunication, and dysfunctional behavior. Chapter 10 concludes with a realistic portrayal of what school communities can achieve when renewal becomes a permanent condition of school life.

We believe what we offer in this book can be useful to teachers, building administrators, superintendents, school board members, community groups, scholars, and policymakers alike, in that we must rethink and reimagine the fundamental ideals of what the American public education system should look like in practice. Whether you agree with what we write is not necessarily the point, but we hope we have stirred up the important philosophical question that has raged since the turn of the 20th century: What is the intent of the American public education system? The future of America depends on our making this shift away from accountability and compliance and toward addressing local issues to help improve the health and vitality of our youth and their communities.

Acknowledgments

This book is dedicated to all those who have maintained that a good school system is one that listens to and addresses the needs of students, parents, and the community more broadly. American history is filled with past, and present, and future (and most often unsung) heroes, including students, faculty, formal school leaders, and community members who have worked hard every day to deliver on the promise of education and public purpose.

Carl D. Glickman
Athens, Georgia
March 2020

Ian M. Mette
Orono, Maine
March 2020

CHAPTER 1

Introduction

Recapturing the Essence of Schools

> "Reinvigorating the civic mission of public education should be the top priority for anyone concerned about the future health of our government and our society."
>
> —Sandra Day O'Connor (2011)

In the following pages we hope to portray the state of our schools, describe the three-dimensional framework of successful schools, and show how public schools, with appropriate involvement and support of local communities and district agencies, can more fully realize their essential purpose. We will also explain how American schools and the American public can stay the course in remaking public schools into moral and productive places for students. The challenge is to deepen the relationship between education and democracy, and this can only be accomplished when schools become vehicles to address the needs of local communities. As Hill (2019) writes about her study of high-quality schools in Boston, "[they] are schools where students are empowered to take leadership responsibility, become civically aware and engaged, and practice decisionmaking so they are prepared to make tough decisions outside of school and into adulthood."

THE FORK IN THE ROAD

Educators have continued through the dizzying events of the past decades to do the best they can for their students, parents, and local community while at the same time dealing with external policies that often have left them confused, anxious, and distressed. There have been more than 2 decades of shifting accountability schemes propelled by the federal legislation of the 2002 policy No Child Left Behind (NCLB) and the 2015 Every Student Succeeds Act (ESSA). This movement focused on common standards and standardized assessments that both highlighted achievement inequities among various student groups and also created a high-stakes testing climate with a hyper-focus on narrowly defined student achievement, test-driven curriculum, and the quantification of teacher evaluation as well as "good teaching." The predicted successful results by policymakers have not materialized (Hess & McShane, 2019).

WHIPPING AMERICAN PUBLIC SCHOOLS WITH EXTERNAL CONTROL

The current generation of young adults is unique. They have only experienced education in the age of highly regulated accountability, which makes their understandings about school control inherently different from previous generations. Schools are less responsible to their own local communities and more driven by bureaucratic dictates and regulations from state and federal policies that operate on a fear basis—threats to take away funding, fire educators, or close a school if students don't achieve at a predetermined level on state standardized tests and other, often shifting, criteria.

The la-la land hopes of policymakers, business leaders, and philanthropists that more standards, more private charter schools, more tests, more frequent and stricter teacher evaluations, and more regulations would create schools that all children would succeed in has been—in the words of wealthy CEO and philanthropist Nick Hanauer (2019), who partnered such efforts with Bill Gates, Alice Walton, and Paul Allen—"tragically misguided." Over these years, there has been an increase in the number of children and adults living in poverty or who are homeless, a decrease in funding for affordable housing, a dramatic increase in opioid use and deaths, and a widening gap in income inequality (Zdenek & Walsh, 2017).

Throughout the last 15 years the American public has continued to focus on the underperformance of public schools, but public schools are simply bellwethers for the health of communities in general. While the hysteria and headlines that public schools are not "producing" student achievement continue, the increasing social needs of communities remain unmet. As unpopular as it is to say, the issue, for many school systems at this point, is not if they are worse than they were before. The issue is whether American public schools are capable of responding to the rising needs of American society more broadly.

People tend to think that their own personal experience, either as a student or with their own children in public schools, makes them an "expert" on what American public education should be. And because of these experiences (which realistically are both positive and negative), American citizens often use this as evidence to complain about the state of American public schools, which account for more of property owners' taxes than any other government service at the local level. As the perennial "whipping boy" for our society, when our country is doing well (the economy is growing and there is little social unrest), Americans do not applaud their schools; they applaud themselves. They extol the American spirit, the can-do economy, the courageous people, and the heroic leaders who remind us to pull ourselves up by our bootstraps. When American society does not do well, however, the American public lambastes our schools. It's a vicious cycle that allows us to compartmentalize the ills of our society rather than having to take a hard look at what is not working well for all Americans.

Schools did not create economic recessions or the decline in American manufacturing. Nor did schools create gun violence, family disintegration, bullying through social media, police brutality, or political upheaval. And yet every day American public schools must live with these realities and try to serve the students that come to them in the best way that they can. In other words, public schools have not undermined the nation's health, as so many reports indicate; rather, we, as a nation, have let our children and our communities down, and this is where the alarm should go off.

In a nation of local, state, and federal governments, there is a lack of attention to and intervention of these conditions, and instead politicians and the American public demand a hyper-focus on student assessment. Rather than supporting student exploration and application of knowledge to respond to these issues at the local level, we have a public school system that currently can only respond to the autocratic demands of state- and federal-level bureaucracies. Due to these stressors, the result has been strain, tension, and an inadequate response on the part of educators and schools to meet the needs of students and parents in their communities. To put it simply, we need to recapture the essence of public schools for the health of our community, the future of our society, and the preservation of our democracy.

BEING REAL

At this point you might say, "My school is not dealing with the same struggles as what is being portrayed here." And this might be true—your community might not be dealing with issues of police brutality or gun violence—but every school is dealing with *some* societal issue(s) from the community that permeates the school walls. The problem, then, is not that American public education is horrible. The problem is that schools are expected to be "cookie-cutter" based on an outdated factory model that promotes compliance and reproduction. Instead, schools should strive for innovation, civil engagement, and application of knowledge in creative ways that can directly translate to better community outcomes. In order to make a shift away from a system of knowledge reproduction to one that promotes civic engagement and contributes to solutions that address societal concerns, we first have to acknowledge that we have lost sight of our top accountability priority.

The problem with American public education is that we have allowed ourselves to become complacent with the current ideology of standardization. We have attempted to standardize our schools, our teachers, our students, and even our communities. Yet those of us who work with students every day know this approach does not work. We see it in the students who become bored with the repetition and monotonous instruction (Mehta & Fine, 2019). We observe it with our fellow teachers who become demoralized with initiatives and prepackaged curriculum and who choose to leave teaching as a result. We feel it when we allow ourselves to be vulnerable and we realize there is very little we can do to help our students who are struggling with real-world problems.

The issue is not how to lift public schools out of disaster—countless great teachers exist within our American schools who would like to do more to help their communities. Instead, the issue is how to allow great schools to exist and help their community thrive, to enable our schools to strive for greatness rather than standardization, and to engage in community building. To do this, however, we need to be real about what it will take to make our schools and communities better. There are no easy solutions, there are no quick fixes, and the responsibility of creating good education does not lie with the state or federal government—it belongs to each local school and the community it serves. What we need to do is reestablish the purpose of public schools and stick to foundation principles of education.

RECAPTURING THE GOAL OF AMERICAN PUBLIC SCHOOLS

In order to recapture the goal of the American public school system, we must first address our current primary goal, which has been to produce results on standardized tests. The problem is this goal often serves the interests of those with the most political, economic, and social clout. The only way to rectify the situation is to make it clear that there is only one primary goal for American public schools: to return to its essence and serve communities by preparing students to become productive citizens of our democracy.

One might quibble with the wording, but the significant elements are there: *service*, *citizenship*, and *democracy*. The goal of American schools is not to be first internationally in mathematics or science, or to send all students to college, or to push students into AP classes. At best, these might be *some* of the sub goals of the larger, single goal of public education, but they do not represent a singular value of our education system. The goal is to create a public education system that helps make our country stronger by providing a wide variety of educational options for students and to apply the skills and knowledge they learn in our schools directly in their community and to our society more broadly.

What is needed is a return to the reason why common schools were established in the first place, why such schools were publicly funded, why the Constitution delegated control of public education away from the federal government, and why an educated citizenry was essential to the working of the Constitution and the Bill of Rights. The value that unites Americans as a people, regardless of religion, culture, race, gender, sexual orientation, identity, lifestyle, socioeconomic class, or political ideology, is a belief in "government of the people, by the people, and for the people." Public education is the only institution designated and funded as the agent of the larger society in protecting the core value of its citizens: democracy. That said, it is time for public education systems to rethink and reimagine the role they could play in helping society more directly address issues of social justice and inequities.

The essential value of the public school system in a democracy, from the beginning, was to ensure an educated citizenry capable of participating in discussions, debates, and decisions to further the wellness of the larger community and protect the individual right to "life, liberty, and the pursuit of happiness." Theoretically, an educated citizenry and a democracy were one and the same; the lack of one would imperil the other. For the last two decades, the public schools of America have been forced to respond to federal and now state requirements that often do little to address issues of inequity surrounding race, ethnicity, socioeconomic, and other cultural factors. Where our public school system has strayed is in its loss of focus on this central goal. And it shows in how we engage each other on social media, in political debates, and among peers.

What difference does it make if we graduate 100% of our students, or if SAT scores rise 20 points, or if our students beat other countries in achievement in science when they have not learned how to identify, analyze, and solve the problems that face their immediate and larger communities? Our country would be better served by schools that produce caring, intelligent, and wise citizens who willingly engage in the work of a democracy and address issues of social justice than by schools that produce graduates who do well on isolated metrics such as standardized achievement scores. There is so much more to our democracy than what we have become hyper-focused on. In many ways, the fate of our country's future might largely depend on our ability to alter what we teach and value in our public school system.

If our schools can recapture their essence, then the expectations and indicators of success will become clearer and our schools will have a moral compass. If our schools were to focus on the main goals of service and citizenship and democracy, and show students how to connect learning with the real issues of their surroundings, then more students would learn how to write cogent compositions, apply skills learned in school to their real-world context, use higher-order thinking, learn aesthetic appreciation, excel in academics, and graduate. These secondary goals would be accomplished more readily as by-products of learned participation and responsibility. The reason why many of our students do not do better in schools is not that they are intellectually deficient, or that their teachers are incompetent or uncaring; the reason is that these students do not see the relevance of such learning to altering and improving their immediate lives in their families and communities more broadly. For them, school learning is a bore or, as one astute student told us, "a hassle you put up with during the day until you can return to the real world." If the central goal of schools were to prepare students to engage productively in a democracy, then this student, with his peers and teachers, would be working on the concerns of his immediate and future life and on the issues facing his community. He would be learning to converse and study; read and write; and understand mathematics, science, art, and music in order to gain the power to make a better life for himself and the people around him.

A cynic might say, "That is all well and good for underachieving and poor students, but what does this 'service and citizenship and democracy' notion have to do with students from highly educated and wealthy homes who do well in school?" The answer is the same. Academically, most privileged students in our public schools do as well as, if not better than, previous generations. Nevertheless, in the absence of the school's central mission, there is only a pro forma experience of doing well, acquiring high grades, and entering a good college so as to get on eventually with life. School for these students is simply a pleasant enough stop on the way to the good life, not an experience that challenges and demands their full mental, emotional, and aesthetic involvement. To be blunt, public education without the central goal of democracy and citizenship is a hollow experience that serves no one well. The ultimate losers are all of us.

The most important ember of an idea that still exists in our American public school system today—protecting freedom in a democracy—was the most revolutionary idea at its inception. Today, it requires that we stoke the idea back into our schools, and breathe life back into democratic ideals of our system, in order to make sure our country can roar into the 21st century. Apathy in the United States and the isolation of students from the life of society are partly the result of our schools' forgetting their essential mission. Public schools that recapture it can move with a fervor, excitement, and engagement that set them apart from the ordinary and the mundane.

A REFRAMING OF THE WORK

If you are a principal, teacher, paraprofessional, parent, student, community member, district official, school board representative, or local policymaker, you already know the solutions to making our schools more democratic will not be easy. We openly acknowledge that we don't offer quick and easy solutions that will help your school system better serve your community. However, *you* have these answers already inside of you. No longer is it appropriate to wait for someone to save your school—that task is yours alone.

In advocating for the local school as the site for decisionmaking and resource allocation, we must also relearn what it means to work closely with community groups and organizations. We must reimagine and reenvision our school systems to serve as the hub for community development. As such, we must not shy away from the societal problems that are dark or scary or traditionally taboo—instead, we must embrace them, as the health of our communities directly impacts the health and vitality of the children we hope to serve in our schools.

ORDINARY GOOD PEOPLE DOING EXTRAORDINARY GOOD WORK

In the latter part of this book, we will discuss the state and national policies that we will need in staying the course of the renewal of public schools. In Chapter 2, we begin with what we have: people in our public schools, with limited time and resources, trying to do their best in constrained conditions. We will move into the "skin" of a public school, lay out the three-dimensional framework of school renewal, and learn how operations and activities can be changed to afford good education to all students.

We are at a fork in the road in America. The path we choose will have an enormous impact on the future of our youth and the future of our society. One path is to acquiesce to the way things are by accepting large inequities among success and failure rates of groups of students—that some people win, some people lose, and the be-all and end-all of education is scores on standardized tests. The other path would be consistent with why many educators choose to go into teaching, for the intellectual and joyful challenge of helping young people to learn to be free through critical thinking, creativity, and problem solving.

Books are written sequentially—from left to right and in numbered chapters. The problem with such a sequential arrangement is that it flies in the face of reality. So even though you read sequentially the chapters about developing the promise, the pledge, and the problem-solving process, you and your colleagues should select a realistic and practical order most suited to the needs of your school and community. We will expand on these different orders in the final chapters.

Part I

A RENEWED FRAMEWORK FOR DEMOCRATIZING SCHOOLS FROM THE INSIDE OUT

CHAPTER 2

The Promise
Establishing Common Principles of Teaching and Learning

Successful organizations and groups, regardless if they exist in the private or public sector of our society, have a set of principles, values, and beliefs that serve as the glue to bring together individuals from a wide variety of backgrounds and experiences. In many ways, this set of beliefs helps move us beyond our egoism to take part in something that is bigger than ourselves, an important ideological consideration in our pro-individualistic American society. However, the transcendent beliefs of successful groups are not forced on individual members, but rather are developed through ongoing dialogue *and* celebrated evidence that what has been (and can be) accomplished together is greater than what could be accomplished alone. As a result, high-functioning groups take part in ongoing goal setting and activities to fulfill both individual and group needs (Johnson & Johnson, 2017).

In American PK–12 public schools, we have a commitment to support the development of our students academically *and* societally. This requires educators to maintain a high level of focus on quality of instruction, but equal consideration must be given to pedagogical and human development considerations. There are plenty of examples of "successful" organizations that are not considered moral or good—some of which have taken part in criminal, discriminatory, or otherwise harmful activities. Think of any number of school districts that have been caught cheating on standardized tests because of the perceived pressure to perform highly on these assessments. If success is the group's accomplishment of its *intended* purposes, then success is neutral in the realm of higher values. Clearly, schools should strive for high student achievement, but not at the expense of developing students who can think critically, be adaptive learners, and apply knowledge in real time to meet the needs of their changing communities and American society in general. A good school is a successful organization that strives to realize the higher values required to prepare productive citizens for a democracy.

SCHOOLS AS SUCCESSFUL ORGANIZATIONS

Unlike other professions and institutions that have a high level of control on the focus and composition of their clientele, the resources that are allocated for use, and the activities they choose to take part in, schools are unique in that they have much less control over these aspects of organizational life. As educators we are unlike most other professions in that we are not internally governed but rather dictated to by outside mandates and requirements. Further complicating our profession is that we do a poor job of building in scheduled time to discuss and plan how we will meet organizational goals *as a group*, and because of this we often are relegated to our own learning silos, typically constrained by the four walls that comprise individual classrooms.

For the purposes of this book, we define successful schools as systems that set their own educational goals and priorities based on the needs of the community they serve and within district, state, and federal legal parameters, and that are able to accomplish these goals over a period of time *for and with* the help of local stakeholders. These goals should include student achievement, grades, and attendance—but they should also include social–emotional learning, increasing access and equity of placement to honors and AP courses, and parental and community satisfaction, among others. Below we offer insights from successful schools where practitioners have begun to bridge the theory–practice gap to create more equitable education systems capable of bettering our American democracy.

Insight 1: Faculty in successful schools constantly look for opportunities to improve their instruction, explicitly targeting inequities of access and achievement. Effective school systems are never complacent with the instructional practices used to engage students and are constantly reflecting on how to improve access for all students. This requires a nuanced approach to improving instruction, where blame is not placed on either the student or the teacher for potential low performance, but rather an access to equity is the focal point of the reflection (Blount, 2013).

Explanation: School systems that are constantly questioning instructional practices are not interested in placing blame for high or low achievement, but rather in rectifying inadequacies created by society or possibly previous actions made within the school system. In other words, being dissatisfied with current practices should not be seen as a weakness—rather, it is a strength of a successful school system that helps drive long-term goals to improve learning. Schools that only celebrate successes or even fail to identify opportunities for improvement divert themselves from the difficult work of making their communities stronger through their own self-reflective processes.

Insight 2: Successful schools de-privatize instructional practices through peer observation, nonjudgmental feedback, and by making curriculum connections across subject areas. There is a growing body of research that suggests the old method of improving instruction, whereby the principal gives directive feedback to teachers about how to improve their instruction, is broken. Learning about instruction with peers helps teachers transform tacit knowledge into explicit knowledge, which allows educators to have conversations about instruction that challenge beliefs and habits, but perhaps most importantly values peers as conversation partners (Knight, 2016).

Explanation: In successful schools, faculty accept the need to have conversations about instructional beliefs and values, as well as ending the privatizing of practices by encouraging peer observation to reflect on other possible pedagogical practices. The goal of this kind of reflection is not to demand compliance with curricular implementation or predetermined pacing guides, but rather to engage in conversations about different possible types of instruction and how curriculum covered might be interconnected across multiple subject areas. Successful schools avoid what has been referred to as contrived collegiality (Datnow, 2011; Hargreaves, 1994), which is administratively determined and compulsory. Instead, successful schools focus on meaningful conversations about instructional observations and how to support each other in improving the educational experience for all students in a school.

Insight 3: Successful schools attempt to flatten the traditional hierarchy of schools as much as possible, empowering teachers to help make decisions regarding the success of their students and encouraging administrators to be mindful of their leadership decisions. In their organizational theory book detailing the importance of creating a culture that deliberately develops every employee, Kegan and Lahey (2016) found that groups that are the most successful in reaching organizational goals value intertwining personal development with organizational development. This requires administrators who are mindful of their leadership, specifically the need to motivate and inspire others to take part in the decisionmaking process within school systems (Goleman, Boyatzis, & McKee, 2013).

Explanation: Successful schools realize in order to further the development of the organization as a whole, personal development and autonomy must also be respected. Successful school systems model what it means to exist in a democratic system, where participation in improving the school system is required of all members of the organization. Additionally, administrators of successful schools are aware of the role they play, not just in helping influence and implement policy and practice but in inspiring all educators to participate in the ongoing school improvement process.

Insight 4: Faculty members, administrators, and others in successful schools establish and protect a culture that is built around having open conversations regarding beliefs and values to constantly review and improve the learning environment for all students. School culture is as important to address as instructional practices (Gruenert & Whitaker, 2015), as negative culture will often inhibit the ability of a school to improve student achievement. As a result, "the way we do things around here" can help or hurt the ability of a school system to reflect on beliefs and values, depending on how democracy is valued within the decisionmaking process of the school culture.

Explanation: Successful schools help keep larger, more philosophical notions about educational practices alive, such as reflecting on our "responsibility to help build a fair and democratic society" (Doddington, 2018, p. 382). Instead of considering how they will maintain high scores on state standardized tests, successful schools also consider what they should do to make their systems more equitable for all students, address issues of social justice, and consider how they can work collaboratively with stakeholders to review the value their system provides to their local community. As a result, successful schools forgo outdated parochial, paternal, or maternal attitudes with earnest discussion about what the members of a school community should be doing together for students.

Insight 5: Successful schools don't merely consume accountability information about their system, but rather they actively produce information about their ongoing renewal process to influence the narrative regarding their education organization. Successful schools are always in the mode of change and renewal. They watch other successful schools at work and keep abreast of the research on topics and activities being considered. They collect data on their students and educational programs, and thus they set priorities that are based on thoughtful study. Perhaps most importantly, successful schools establish meaningful partnerships between schools and families that encourage deep learning about real problems that instills a desire to "help humanity" (Fullan, 2016, p. 11).

Explanation: Most schools' goals and priorities are afterthoughts to external directives for school improvement plans. Such goals and priorities usually come from the decisions of a few individuals or from surveys of faculty members and address change at the most surface of levels. Successful schools operate at a much deeper level by seriously studying the needs of their students and communities, and making changes to their programs with the input of stakeholders and not simply as a closed system. Successful schools "deconstruct knowledge frameworks that perpetuate an inequitable status quo and . . . [instead] promote inclusion and equity" (Shields, 2014,

p. 128). With this in mind, school renewal is an ongoing, everyday occurrence that is influenced by the narrative it creates between a school system and the community it serves.

TRADITIONS OF (MIS)EDUCATION

So, what should we make of these five insights about successful schools? If nothing more, they should be a reminder of what schools *can accomplish* if not hampered with unnecessary accountability structures. Successful schools are places of learning—for both children *and* adults—where people come together to continually reflect on what it might take for a community to make living conditions better than what existed a generation before. The answers are never the same from one community to another, nor can the solutions be a once-and-for-all framework. Most importantly, the best answers come from those closest to the problems of the community, not from an outside source with little to no context of local issues.

While it might appear to some that the solutions to all of our problems in American PK–12 public education might simply require some common sense, it is important to acknowledge that the solutions to many of our challenges are in fact messy, undefined, and challenging to transform from ideas into actions (Fahey, Breidenstein, Ippolito, & Hensley, 2019; Glickman, Allen, & Lunsford, 1994). Some schools have risen above the pressures of the accountability era; however, many are just starting to realize the damage this has done to our schools and how our thinking about student learning has been altered.

Most of our schools have felt powerless and have succumbed to the "teach to the test" ideology that prevents them from acknowledging and addressing the needs of their communities. This acquiescence to external authority and accountability puts our democracy at risk, in how we think about responding to local needs and also what is needed to rethink student success and the structures of our school system, as well as the historical inequities that are deep-seeded parts of American society.

So, what is it about our American PK–12 public education system that prevents us from changing an outdated organizational model? How might we refocus on how to make our education systems more democratic (Dewey, 1916)? Perhaps most importantly, why is it difficult for educators to make changes in real time, changes that would benefit students and help us make our schools and communities better? We discuss a few of the reasons in the following sections on why it is so difficult to change our current system.

Remnants of the Industrial Model

If one were to build a structure whose purpose was the production of standardized outputs, it would look like either a school or a factory. Both run on bell systems, both have multiple layers of hierarchy to evaluate the performance of subordinates, and both departmentalize in an attempt to implement quality control of a product or output. And yet we know that successful companies and businesses often do not run like a factory model. Many companies have shifted to open floor plans with common work areas to share ideas and talk about work tasks and flow, all to be able to learn from each other and improve their product. However, our schools still utilize an egg crate structure, with one teacher to approximately 20 or 30 students, where each teacher is boxed off from other teachers and is unable to see the work of her/his peers. Additionally, many schools still struggle to create a schedule that provides embedded common planning times for informal or formal meetings. As many educators know, the schedule dictates what we are able to do in class, and in this case, the physical space also determines why it is so difficult to respond to the ever-changing needs of students in real time.

Infiltration of the American Education Industry

Since the 1980s, the American PK–12 public education system has been increasingly influenced by policymakers to utilize more business management approaches in the attempt to increase the efficiency of schools (Peck & Reitzug, 2012). School Improvement Grants (SIGs) and Race to the Top (RTTT) funding have not only acted as economic levers to change policies and practices of schools to make them function more like a business, but have also created ample opportunities for third-party vendors to access market revenue. In the 2013–2014 school year, $634 billion was generated in total expenditures for public elementary and secondary schools (NCES, 2017a), highlighting just how large a sector public education has become. Almost any public school system selected today will likely have one or more prepackaged curricula it is implementing, as these curricula are highly aligned to the state test. Add in teacher evaluation systems, social–emotional curriculum, and professional development for teachers, and you can see that it would be difficult to disrupt such an established economic system that offers so many prepackaged solutions to school reform problems.

Restricted Thinking About Learning

Educators have been increasingly told their students must regurgitate information on a single high-stakes test if they are to be considered successful by public measure. However, as school systems have been consistently reinforced to value rote memorization, the most successful corporations and organizations in the world have increasingly not valued this type of thinking or learning. Instead, highly successful organizations (e.g., Google, Apple, Microsoft) value the *application and creation* of new knowledge to either create new markets or solve existing social issues. As a result, schools often have a limited and/or restricted view about what and how they teach, as well as how students will apply knowledge once they graduate.

Increasingly, schools also have restricted views and beliefs about adult learning as well. Many use prepackaged evaluation systems (e.g., Marzano, Danielson, Marshall, etc.) that place teachers on a continuum rather than valuing supervisory conversations that empower teachers to drive their own reflection and learning about instruction (Glickman, Gordon, & Ross-Gordon, 2018). What results is the continuation of top-down feedback about performance by principals, central office administrators, school boards, state departments, legislatures, and governors rather than the encouragement of teachers to challenge and question what is being taught and how this impacts the lives of students. From this, we see schools that place importance on autocratic values, which results in a void of democratic ideals, beliefs, and a general lack of understanding about the value of creative thinking and learning.

Lack of Professional Dialogue

Schools struggle to take part in meaningful dialogue and conversations about professional practices, and as a result often resort to traditional forms of hierarchy rather than viewing themselves as a social system (Mette & Riegel, 2018; Schein, 2010). Most educators do not discuss teaching practices with one another except in contrived situations, and rarely do these form the content of faculty meetings, lounge conversations, or hallway exchanges. Usually, principals and teachers are more comfortable discussing students, parents, sports events, or community matters than discussing such issues as curriculum implementation, teaching strategies, staff development, and student learning. And yet many educators want the opportunity to be able to discuss these important matters, but lack the time, space, or structure to engage in conversations that allow for reflection, inquiry, and deepening of self-efficacy.

EXISTING CONDITIONS AS A FORUM FOR DISCUSSION: TYPES OF SCHOOLS

The traditions of schools we just reviewed are not sinister conspiracies about our American PK–12 public education system; however, they reveal the challenges we face if we are to make our schools more democratic and capable of meeting the needs of local communities. We want to be clear that schools are less than fully effective not because educators are uncaring—quite the opposite, in fact. There are very few teachers and administrators who take or even have coffee breaks or spend their school time in idle leisure. The overwhelming majority of educators work extremely hard, without great pay and often in pressure-cooker conditions. Perhaps most importantly, we know that most educators strive to do the very best they can for their students. And yet it is the structure we have adopted (and has been imposed) in the age of accountability that has often prevented us from being more effective.

Educators are often caught unwittingly in structures and conventions that are counterproductive to the improvement of teaching practices. Teachers and principals are good people who try to do good work, but who have become tired and at times discouraged because they simply cannot make the existing system work any better for themselves or their students (You & Conley, 2015). The issue becomes one of building a school community where members have an opportunity to rethink the existing organization and decide on the level of energy and activity at which they wish to change schoolwide teaching and learning practices. This is not to be taken lightly: As people rethink their organization and its purpose, function, and activities, they move outside the secure and the known. While changing students' lives, they will be changing their own lives as well. In our own work with schools that are engaged in such rethinking, we have witnessed the experience to be both exhilarating and painful. Once begun, however, it is hard to turn back.

Table 2.1 shows three types of school organization: neo-conventional, congenial, and collegial. *Neo-conventional* schools are characterized by the industrial model mentality of education: isolated practice with little opportunity to observe other instruction, district-mandated and controlled implementation of curriculum, and lack of self-efficacy in terms of implementing personal beliefs about instructional practices in order to meet the individual needs of students. *Congenial* schools are characterized by an open, social climate for adults, where people have high levels of autonomy but schoolwide practices, beliefs, or ideologies are not discussed or challenged. Communications are friendly, and teachers, parents, caretakers, and principals easily socialize with one another. Faculty meetings are pleasant,

Table 2.1. Types of Schools

Neo-Conventional	Congenial	Collegial
Isolated	Social	Professional respect; personal caring as a by-product of work
District controlled	Individual teacher autonomy valued	Collective autonomy
School seen as implementation of another person's ideas or beliefs	Pleasant and open climate for adults as long as no one is challenged	Purposeful conversation about practices, conflicts are seen as valued, resolution determined on behalf of students and community

holiday parties are great, refreshments at meetings are plentiful, and faculty members spend time together away from school (yoga on Thursday night, weekly happy hours, etc.). Members describe their school as a nice place where everyone gets along well, but the status quo is not challenged.

Collegial schools, on the other hand, are characterized by purposeful, adult-level interactions focused on the teaching and learning of both students and adults. People do not necessarily socialize with one another, but they respect their differences of opinion about education and create time to reflect on these ideals. Mutual professional respect comes from the belief that everyone has the students' interests in mind, and that there are many ways to meet the needs of students. The result of this respect is seen in school meetings, where the school community members debate, disagree, and argue before educational decisions are made. Even in the hottest of debates, people's professional respect for others supersedes personal discomfort. People believe that differences will be resolved and that students will benefit as a result of the discomfort. Social satisfaction is a by-product of professional engagement and resolution, of seeing how students benefit, and of the personal regard in which adults hold one another. They become colleagues in the deep sense of being able to work and play together, and each side of the relationship strengthens the other. Being collegial means being willing to move beyond the social facade of communication, to discuss conflicting ideas and issues with candor, sensitivity, and respect. For many schools, the first job is to move from being neo-conventional to being congenial, but the big challenge for public education is to become collegial, so that social satisfaction is derived mainly from the benefits resulting from efforts addressing issues of social inequities and injustices on behalf of students. Without this, educators cannot work together to help their school be more democratic.

Without a clear understanding of the primary goal of schools—fostering citizenship in a democracy—and an ensuing promise about teaching and learning, a school may easily take on greater collective decisionmaking, building a structure and making time for it, but still be no better a place for students or the community. Instead, people may make decisions that improve the lives of adults (a better adult climate, more socially cohesive activities) rather than making decisions that improve teaching and learning, as well as addressing the problems that exist at the local or neighborhood level impacting students who attend a school. Ultimately, the aim is to have a school environment that fulfills students' needs, educators' needs, and the needs of a community.

DEVELOPING THE PROMISE

The idea that public education and democracy are intertwined creates the central goal for the American PK–12 public school system. For schools to be true to that goal, procedures and processes for its accomplishment must be democratic. This point touches on the glaring hypocrisy of public school operations and on why policymakers have fallen short in sustaining strategies and reforms for improving education. Most policies in public education are undemocratic in their creation and implementation. Policies are not decided by those who will be affected, do not represent the people in the school or the local community more broadly, and are not derived from the vision of the people the school serves. Most ideas in education derive from power, popularity, or novelty. These ideas temporarily hold sway, but within a few years they pass away and become tried innovations that failed. Then critics of the American PK–12 public school system have yet another field day with the failure of our schools, when in fact the issue is we live in a country with glaring issues of inequity and we do little to address these problems, either because they are too difficult to solve or it makes different groups of Americans uncomfortable to admit the "system" doesn't work for everyone.

For school renewal to endure, every school and district in our land needs principles that transcend the interests of any individual and that are derived from constituents. These principles must be congruent with a definition of the core values of a democracy: freedom, justice, and equality *as well as* life, liberty, and the pursuit of happiness *for all*. And all means all—regardless of race, class, identity, orientation, or background. These principles will not be swayed by politics, fads, or special interests. Such a promise, rather than taking up space in a policy book or passing someone else's inspection, is a living embodiment of why we as a school community do what we do. It becomes the rallying cry for saying "Yes, we value you and the experiences you bring!" or the defensive response, "No, that's not how we do things around here."

We use the word *promise* purposely here, to describe learning principles that are derived from a definition of education and democracy and that are more than a vision of teaching and learning. A vision is what we would like to imagine; a promise is an oath and obligation to serve something greater than ourselves. A promise should be reconsidered and revised periodically, but it is where the heart of a school resides, the place from which it will not be moved. A promise is part of the true American Dream—not one created for and by White men—one that deconstructs the inequities of our society and teaches us how to live with each other and take care of one another. From this dream emanates a mission, goals, and plans.

There are many ways and sequences for establishing a promise, but the important thing is that the promise be: 1) derived from all the people who are affected (including but not limited to students, parents, staff, administrators, community groups, nonprofits, business partners, etc.); 2) derived through a democratic process, whereby no one person makes decisions for everyone else; 3) focused solely on teaching and learning and what teaching and learning should look like in the particular school; and 4) a guide for future decisions about school priorities with respect to such matters as staff, schedules, materials, assessment, curriculum selection and implementation, staff development, and resource allocation, among others.

PRINCIPLES OF LEARNING

The following principles illustrate such a promise (Glickman & Thompson, 2009). These were influenced by the notion of how a Community Learning Exchange (CLE) process can bring together students, parents, educators, community groups, and local stakeholders to determine answers to school and community improvement at the local level (Guajardo, Guajardo, Janson, & Militello, 2016). The question that should guide any discussion about the promise a school makes as a community is "What should learning look like in an optimal educational environment?" We offer the following framework:

1. Learning should be an active process that demands full student participation in pedagogically valid work that values critical thinking. Students need to make choices, accept responsibility, and become self-directed with higher-order thinking and learning opportunities.
2. Learning should be both an individual and a cooperative venture, where students need to work at their own pace and performance levels and also have opportunities to use collaborative learning structures with other students to solve problems facing their local community.
3. Learning should be goal oriented and connected to the real world, so that students understand that the applications of what they learn in school can be directly applied to their lives outside of school.
4. Learning should be personalized, for both students and teachers, to allow both children and adults to learn together, and to set learning goals that are realistic but challenging, attainable, and pertinent to their future aspirations. This requires creating a culture that values vulnerability to identify what can be learned that is not known and then supporting all members of the school to develop an inquiry stance.
5. Learning should be documentable, diagnostic, and reflective, providing continuous feedback to students and parents, to encourage students, and to train them in self-evaluation. Assessment should be used as a tool to develop further teaching and learning strategies.
6. Teaching should be documentable, diagnostic, and reflective, providing continuous feedback to teachers and principals, to

encourage teachers to improve instruction through self-study, peer coaching, and a culture of capacity building.
7. Learning and teaching should take place in a comfortable and attractive physical environment and in an atmosphere of support and respect, where both students' and teachers' own life experiences are affirmed and valued and where mistakes are analyzed constructively as a natural step in the acquisition of knowledge and understanding.

Another promise for teaching and learning can be adapted from this methodology. Students in every classroom, staff members at faculty meetings, and parents and community members at evening meetings are given the same individual task: to describe their most memorable learning experiences. After reminiscing, writing, and narrating in small groups, people are then asked to determine the underlying principles of learning that were common to their most memorable learning experiences. The final step is to ask representatives of each group to come together and determine what learning should look like so that the school can be filled with memorable learning experiences for students today.

Each school will need to adjust the questions and procedures to best fit its own context. Several other questions could also be used for deriving a promise, including but not limited to: What makes a good school? How do you learn best? What would teaching and learning look like in the ideal classroom or school? What is currently missing from instruction in our school? How might we better use the knowledge we teach in our schools to address the concerns of the community? What are the concerns of the community? If you could learn in any way that you wanted, how would you go about it? Of course, very young children, as well as others who have difficulty writing, will have to be able to narrate their ideas to an adult, an older student, or a volunteer. Schools where parents or caretakers do not usually attend meetings may have to be sampled and surveyed by correspondence, phone, or personal visit, or representative parents can be invited to attend a special coffee hour. Students themselves could develop interview protocols and survey grandparents and businesspeople. There is no single way of developing such principles, but they should be derived through a democratic process conducted by those affected to better meet the needs of a community and to address how we can make our schools more democratic.

What has been interesting for us in conducting this type of exercise with various schools, community groups, and stakeholders is how remarkably alike the lists of principles are. People of various political persuasions, economic levels, races, cultures, and ages tend to see optimal learning in generally similar terms. Nevertheless, the differences create insight and discussion about our democracy more broadly, and resolving them contributes to the uniqueness of each school.

WHAT TO DO WITH THE PROMISE

After deriving a promise through a democratic process (more details on school-based democratic procedures will be found in the next chapter), the school now has a framework for comparing desired learning in principle with current day-to-day practices. In such discrepancy checks, a school may immediately find that certain practices (teaching methods, materials, allocation of instructional time, grouping of students, grading and evaluation practices over the normal course of a day) are consistent with the promise, while others are in stark contrast or opposition. It will probably become obvious that there is a need to study what actually happens to students during their school day—what they learn, how they go about learning, and how they apply their learning in a broader context.

The structure for school renewal must be built first, to provide a firm shelter for the "inside" work. One side of the three-part framework—the promise—has now been constructed. The other two sides—the pledge, as well as problem solving via the action research process—remain.

CHAPTER 3

The Pledge
Creating a Commitment to Make Decisions as a Community

No matter how much state and federal reform policies try to force locally controlled school districts to implement new school improvement efforts, nothing will lead to increased student outcomes until we as educators realize we belong to communities rather than the other way around. For the better part of 15 years, accountability measures have sent the message that school systems, and what is done in school systems, is determined by state or federal government policies. Yet experienced educators know that students cannot be reached unless learning is relevant to them and their family, and that it is the responsibility of a school to promote community, not control community. Faculty, staff, and administrators need to relearn, reimagine, and reconceptualize the intent of the American school system.

Students do not "belong" to one teacher, nor can student achievement in one subject be held accountable to one teacher. What schools are accountable for is the formal education of the young over the course of many years; and while they are members of a school district, students are first members of a larger community—something that connects them in crucial ways beyond the classroom walls. And we cannot help students understand the power of education, and what it might afford them socially, economically, and politically, unless we teach them the foundations of how an activated democracy works within society.

As such, we need to move past a fragmented education system where students learn academic subjects in isolation rather than applied to their own understanding about themselves, their community, and the world they will inherit. We as educators need to reimagine an education system for our students, one that moves beyond the comparisons of mine vs. yours, struggling vs. smart, rich vs. poor, Black/Brown vs. White.

In order to envision what our schools can be—places of learning that belong to everyone and are accountable to the community they serve—a collective pledge is essential.

DEVELOPING A DECISIONMAKING PROCESS

A pledge is a commitment to a decisionmaking process of the school-based community. It acknowledges social, racial, and economic inequities, and creates a pact between peoples of varying backgrounds and experience to contribute to the improvement of a community.

The pledge acknowledges old wounds, helps to heal painful pasts, and develops an education vision of a better world for our children as we prepare them for adulthood. The decisionmaking process includes determining the following: 1) who is considered in the development of the pledge, 2) what will be the actions and processes used to increase a democratic system, 3) when will there be time to take part in the creation and implementation of such a pledge, 4) where will the outcomes of this work be measured, 5) why is this work important, and 6) how will a community continually assess the value of creating a more democratic school system?

In what follows, we will describe democratic procedures that can lead to higher commitments to the needs of local communities. There is not one specific model to follow to increase democratic principles in our school buildings, but rather what is important is that the process fits the individual school and school system and is more accountable to its community and more broadly to a more participatory and wise democratic society. It is the creation and maintenance of belonging to a community that allows voices to be heard and keeps all of us connected to something bigger than ourselves.

GUIDING RULES OF DECISIONMAKING

There are five guiding rules to increasing democracy in our schools. As basic as they may seem, a surprisingly large percentage of schools *do not* display these governing principles, perhaps due to the pressure of mandated accountability and external regulations of the past decades. To increase the democratization of schools, educators should consider the following (adapted from Johnson & Johnson, 2017):

1. Develop clear and relevant goals that create commitment to the community.
2. Establish a communication process to ensure ideas and feelings are heard.
3. Capitalize on structured controversies to challenge conclusions in order to create high-quality decisions.
4. Ensure conflicts are mediated and resolved constructively.
5. Once decisions are made, everyone agrees to support the implementation.

To be an active member of society at large, we first need to understand what it means to function productively in a group, as well as to put these ideals into action. Just because we are part of a group does not mean we are required to take part in its decisionmaking process; however, if we abdicate our voice, time, and effort to take part in a democratic group process, we cannot complain about the implementation of what the group as a whole has decided. For example, if our town or city holds a special referendum to vote on a school bond or to raise taxes and we do not exercise our voice and vote, then we only have ourselves to blame about the failure of passage of the issue. The same is true in the decisionmaking process of our school systems. The time to make our views known is during the process. Afterward, we can grumble and try to have the decision reconsidered; in the meantime, we must abide by it.

The strength of having these guiding rules of decisionmaking in a school system is that they do not force people to be involved in decisions that they may not have the time, interest, or energy to be invested in. Additionally, the rules support the sharing of ideas and feelings, as well as addressing controversies and the mediation of conflicts. What they provide is a framework for a group of people, educators, parents, students, and community members to commit themselves to the process of decisionmaking that will increase democratic participation and make their community better. An individual who does not like a particular decision but who choses not to be involved in the decisionmaking process will learn to become more involved in the future.

LOCUS OF CONTROL

In order for a democracy to be effective, the governance system needs to a) address issues that are of importance to the people involved in making decisions, b) be made by people who are closely impacted by the decisions being made, and c) empower those invested to make changes that will improve the lives of people now.

Schools and districts can only control their own spheres of influence, and as such need to establish governance structures that address "what we can do" in "our own school" and that are "within our control." If parameters can be established at the local level, there will be a far greater investment by faculty, staff, parents, and volunteer community members and far better learning outcomes for students.

The locus of control within schools always has, and always will be, what *we* can do—not what *others* think we should do—within the authority and policies developed at the local level. Of course, there will still be state requirements in terms of certification, school safety, and appropriate use of funding. That said, there needs to be greater delineation between what a community values for student outcomes and what a district, state, or federal government says should be achieved on a standardized test.

In later chapters, we will discuss the need for coordination, decentralization, new district board and state policies, and private–public partnerships that help improve the quality of living for all students. For now, the simple message is that a school community must decide for itself what type of teaching and learning place it wants to be. Since educators are trained professionals, the time we spend on governance should be spent on what can be done and attained, rather than on what cannot be controlled.

FACTORS IMPACTING DEMOCRACY IN SCHOOLS

If a school system is focused on the public purpose of education that can strengthen our own democracy as a country, the school itself must serve as an example of a functioning democracy. It is one thing to say "We want to improve democracy in our schools!," but quite another to ensure this is translated into action. As such, we need to consider factors that will help enact the promise: how to build a stronger culture, focus on actions and beliefs that directly impact student learning, increase community engagement, and develop district-level support structures to continually foster a high-quality school system focused on learning and applied to democratic principles.

What does this all mean? How might we better focus on high-quality instruction, meaningful learning, and the vision of a school system that can be true to its promise? For the work of schools to return to the strengthening of our democracy, we must rethink our vision, our purpose, and the actions and structures that are most helpful in supporting a school to be a democratic and educative community. Table 3.1 shows these types of beliefs and practices that are factors impacting how democratic a school is and can be and the type of learning that can occur.

The factors of the culture of a school community tell us where we are and where we hope to be in furthering the democratization of education. Factors such as how open a school is to inviting visitors into the building, the amount of input (or lack thereof) teachers have in equally distributing noninstructional duties, and the conversations that are held in the faculty lounges or workrooms (particularly to prevalence of negative talk about students) all play a vital role in understanding the tasks to make a school more democratic and less authoritarian. Additionally, the more authentic and trusting the relationships are between the adults of the school, the better the educational experience can be created and provided for students. These factors might seem inconsequential, but they play a crucial role in the foundation of trust and teamwork and reducing the "I blame you" game we have come to see so often over the last decade and a half.

Table 3.1. Factors Impacting Democracy and Learning

Culture of a School Community	Building Beliefs and Actions Impacting Student Learning	Community Engagement Structures and Activities	District Support Structures to Maximize Democracy
Openness to invite others into a school building	Individualized and building-wide staff development	Parent-led programs (e.g., PTA)	Ability to hire high-quality teachers and staff
Teacher input in the sharing of "other duties as assigned"	Coaching and peer feedback systems to promote reflection	Use of community leaders as guest speakers	Leadership development of principles and leadership feedback
Types of discussions held in faculty lounge	Use of data to drive enrichment and remediation	Locally determined accountability measures	Passing a school budget that promotes instructional equity
Authentic relationships among adults of the school	Purposeful connections between curriculum and application	Use of student learning within the community	Creating space for the community to be part of the school system

Building beliefs and actions impacting student learning are critical factors that will impact democratic actions within a school building. Focusing on individualized, as well as building-wide, staff development provides an opportunity for teachers to learn more about themselves as well as what it means to be a contributing team member of a school system. Additionally, democratic schools are able to de-privatize instruction through the use of instructional coaches and peer feedback systems that value observation and develop instructional reflection stances. Using data to drive enrichment and remediation activities, as well as ensuring a purposeful connection between curriculum and real-world application, are belief structures that require educators to come together in a democratic fashion and consider, together, how to bridge what is being learned, internalized, and then used immediately in a local context.

Community engagement structures and activities are about factors that go beyond traditional parental engagement. Parent-Teacher Association (PTA) collaboration is still important, but other factors—such as regularly bringing in community leaders as guest speakers, bringing in stakeholders from across the community on a yearly basis to determine and update locally determined accountability measures, offering family engagement activities around school events, and the use of student learning within the community—deepen the importance and impact of democracy in our schools. Without these activities, schools remain a closed system, when they should be an open system that has a symbiotic relationship with the community it serves.

District support structures to maximize democracy have the least day-to-day impact on student learning but are perhaps the most important to improving the long-term impact of support for the democratization of a school system. It starts with the ability of the school district to hire high-quality teachers and staff as well as the commitment to focus on the leadership development of principals and providing timely feedback on their leadership. District support is also crucial in terms of modeling democratic principles and helping craft, support, and pass a school budget that promotes instructional equity in the 21st century. That said, it is also the responsibility of district-level leaders to create space for the community to be part of the school system and to help navigate the politics that might be involved when increasing democratic principles in a school system.

THE IDEAL GOVERNING RULES

The question of who should sit at the table and have an equal say in educational decisions is simultaneously complicated and simple. Ideally, all those involved in an education system should have voting membership. Educational decisions at the school level will affect faculty, the principal, students, staff, paraprofessionals, parents and caretakers, other community members, businesspeople, district office personnel, and school board members. Furthermore, subgroups within each category of membership could be broken down even further. For example, faculty could be subdivided into core subject teachers, elective teachers, special education teachers, paraprofessionals, and other support personnel. They also could be subdivided by upper grade, lower grade, department, gender, years of experience, and so on. Such subdivision can be taken to impractical extremes, however, and for some can be seen as hurtful, divisive, exclusive (if a group is not represented), and exactly the problem we are currently witnessing in our own elected officials in terms of who gets to make decisions, how, and why. Taking great care to include any and all who want to participate, and revisiting these groups, is crucial.

Below we provide the ideal ground rules for school governance group membership:

1. All major groups should be represented, with access always open to others who might want to join.
2. Teachers should be the majority when considering pedagogical decisions.
3. Community members should be equally represented when considering local accountability measures and application of learning within the community.

4. Administrators should be standing members (automatically included) but have no more authority in the discussion process of how to implement democratic ideals than any other voting member.
5. The groups should be representative of the school and community as a whole, including but not limited to race, ethnicity, socioeconomic status, and gender.

Rule 1 means that the democratic process should be open to any member of the group (parents, teachers, community members, students), regardless of whether he or she has a formal role on an official governing board. There should be task forces and study groups, with formal solicitations for any interested persons to participate, and open hearings should be held before a formal governing board makes any important schoolwide decision. In this way, anyone in the school community can participate at some level and be heard.

Rule 2 is crucial to school renewal. Teachers should have the majority voice on all decisions affecting their professional work. The work of educators is education—implementing engaging teaching and learning practices. We are aware that some disagree with the idea that teachers should have majority control. If teaching is to ever become a true profession, and perhaps more importantly, if we are to reconnect our school systems to the service of our local communities, then teachers must be able to exercise their own professional judgment. Teachers are prepared on how to teach, to deeply consider pedagogical practices and implications, and to reflect on how each *individual* student learns best, and we need to empower them to be professionals. It is only in allowing teachers to use their minds and collective judgment with other community members that we establish critical, thoughtful, and professionally engaging places that retain, support, and attract thoughtful professionals, in both school systems and the communities they serve more broadly. If educational decisions are to be made by a majority of citizens, laypeople, or noneducators, then we do not need educators. If this were true, and if we want to continue to allow standardized testing to drive the educational experiences of our children, then we might as well eliminate all specialized preparation for teachers and simply hire people who are willing to follow other people's ideas and assessment practices on education. Giving noneducators total control over educational decisions will not improve public schools—in fact, during the accountability movement, we have seen record numbers of teachers leave the profession due to the demoralization of people questioning their professional opinions (Santoro, 2018). All this being said, some school issues are not primarily pedagogically based, and these certainly do call for greater representation by noneducators.

Rule 3 speaks to the importance of greater community involvement and engagement within a school system. This includes issues such as developing local accountability measures determined by a balanced mix of community members and educators, as well as considering how what is being learned in school can be applied and valued in a community context. Additionally, community members are critical in considering and establishing community values, school or community service programs, parent programs, after-school programs, and use of community resources. As these important community-based decisions rise to the surface and are made, a school will, in time, find clarity and consistency with its promise.

Rule 4 means that the school administrators, typically the principal and assistant principal(s), if applicable, should always be viewed as critically important faculty members, with broad responsibility for overall coordination and articulation of school programs. Therefore, the principal is rightfully seen as a permanent member of the school's governing group. This does not necessarily mean that she or he formally convenes and presides over the governing group or has any greater influence than anyone else. Again, some argue the opposite, but in our experience and observation of successful schools, principals only use their formal authority if a faculty is making decisions that hurt students. Principals should not be disenfranchised from the educational operations of teacher-run schools; instead, they should be seen as faculty members who have made the same career commitment as other faculty to improve education for students. In some places, adversarial conditions between principals and teachers (the management–labor dichotomy) have come about through the loss of the original idea of the principal as head *teacher* rather than head *administrator*. Once again, this has been magnified and perpetuated in a dysfunctional accountability climate. We can recapture the sense of principal and teachers as part of the same faculty only if those in education, regardless of their conferred roles, see one another primarily as educators, with the same care, concern, and right to make educational decisions.

Rule 5 states that the group as a whole must reflect the diversity of the community. In a previous edition of this book, we stated that we hoped there would be a day when such a rule would not need to be spoken but would be automatically understood and followed. We have yet to reach that day, and as a result we must fiercely defend this foundation of democracy. If the school and the community represent certain proportions of ethnic and socioeconomic groups, then so should the governing board. If the school has a large percentage of students from low-income households, parents and guardians from low-income households should be represented. If the school community has more women than men, then men should not be overrepresented on the governing board. Paying attention to the issue of representation empowers community members and educators to speak not just to each other but with each other, and to collectively make decisions that will help address cultural, social, and economic issues at the local level.

NAVIGATING BETWEEN IDEAL AND REALITY

The ideal can be embraced all at once or in transitional steps over 2 or 3 years. This is where sensitivity to the school's cultural readiness, beliefs about student learning, prior history with community engagement, and district support come into play. For example, if a school's parent and community group has constantly played a role (positive or negative), then it would make sense to involve those people heavily in decisions about the governing board's composition. If a school has had a noticeable lack of parent or community involvement, it might be equally important to begin with an in-school governing board (consisting mostly of school personnel) and immediately commission a study or advisory group of invited parents and community members to recommend how the governing board might have greater parent or community representation within a few years.

The same holds true for student voice, choice, and representation in school decisions. Students should be represented in school governance, although to what degree continues to be an open debate. A school with younger children, typically grades PK–5, will want to give students more choice and opportunity to discuss, explore, investigate, and create possible solutions to the issues that impact them directly at home, within the walls of the school building, and in the community more broadly. These issues might include, but are not limited to, drug use disorder, observed violence, poverty and trauma, or a variety of other possible social issues personally experienced or observed. The classroom then becomes a learning ground to reflect on and apply concepts taught at grade-appropriate levels to the personal and social issues that are of concern to children. Older students, typically in grades 6–12, should be able to move beyond possible solutions to apply knowledge in action. Older students also have the opportunity to deliver and support information to younger grades as a way to model for students the interconnection of a school system to the community more broadly. Regardless of age, there are critical opportunities for school systems to infuse democratic ideals that provide opportunities for students to be more invested in their own learning, to see their school as a place that is connected to their community, to have a voice in how learning is applied in a real-world context, to commit to their own learning and how knowledge acquisition is valuable, and to develop proper ethical and civic behavior as they progress through a school system.

The proper involvement of central office, district, and school board personnel can also be complicated. Ideally, central office personnel are able to provide feedback to principals in a meaningful way that helps them grow as democratic leaders and promotes self-reflection about leadership decisions and actions more broadly. Additionally, district leaders should be able to help school buildings navigate the political realities of what is required to more deeply connect community members to decisions made within a school building that impacts local constituents. The reality, however, is that in many districts there are not enough people who have the time, inclination, attitude, or expertise to serve in these types of roles. Therefore, the compromise for many schools is they must try to democratize their school building on their own and without ongoing feedback and support. The role, organization, and policies of districts involved in supporting school renewal will be discussed further in later chapters.

The discussion of the gap between the ideal and the reality of composing a governing group in a school is about where it might need to start (the reality) and, eventually, about how the school wishes to be (the ideal). At a minimum, a school needs to start with a majority of school faculty and the principal, with active solicitation of paraprofessionals, students, parents, community members, and district personnel on issues that are relevant to local communities. Eventually, a school's governance should include representatives of all the school's various constituencies.

WHAT TYPE OF GOVERNANCE?

While it might seem that increasing democratic ideals and processes in schools in a structured and straightforward manner would be an easy process, the reality is this is simply not true. Teachers and administrators alike need to take seriously finding a balance between site-based decisionmaking (Glazer, 2009; Meyer, 2009) and how systems-based decisions are made and implemented (Grammatikopoulos, 2012). Increasing democracy can require large time investments by participants, but not giving enough time to voice opinions can also negatively impact the decisionmaking process. As such, schools need to make their own judgments about the best way to increase democracy among their own stakeholders without overloading busy people with issues best handled by other means, and then consistently reflect on how and if the governing process helps improve community outcomes. What is true about democracy in America, and what should always be true, is that everyone can be involved in the decisionmaking process over high-priority schoolwide topics, but that no one *has* to be involved. That said, once a decision is made, everyone must agree to support the implementation or to work through the democratic process to update a decision.

Governing democratic structures typically include some form of the following: 1) one person, one vote; 2) no ultimate veto for any individual; 3) use of a decisionmaking rule that finalizes decisions; and 4) a ratification process and structure by the body at large. "One person, one vote" is fairly self-explanatory. "No ultimate veto" simply means that no one person (including the principal) can permanently make decisions for the group—an ultimate veto only occurs in totalitarian societies and does not belong in the American democracy. If the democratic process is to include veto power—used by the chair of a committee, the principal, or some other form of leadership—it should be a temporary one with the ability to override the veto by a predetermined majority. "Use of a decisionmaking rule to finalize decisions" implies a standing protocol that every member is aware of in order to vote and finalize a decision. This can be simple majority, two-thirds, consensus, or some other rule to resolve issues and move forward with final approval. "Ratification process" is simply the final process in the democratic structure before implementation. In schools, this typically requires a large majority of the faculty (often 60–80%), as well as the support of the superintendent and the school board.

REPRESENTATIVE, DIRECT, AND HYBRID GOVERNANCE

The democratization of schools typically is categorized in three forms: representational democracy, direct participation democracy, or a hybrid of the two. All three have their merits and require different types of participation by local stakeholders. A representative form of democracy means that members of the educational community, including teachers, staff, students, parents, administrators, and community members, are elected or serve as volunteers to represent their particular constituents (see Figure 3.1). Within this democratic structure, representative members make decisions on behalf of their group and consider how this impacts the community more broadly. As such, the "people" of the community are represented through these governing bodies, and while they may be consulted at times, their "say" is given to their respective representatives.

The second form of democracy used in schools is direct participation (see Figure 3.2). Similar to that of a town meeting, anyone can voice their opinion and is required to as there is no representation. Here, people keep their "say" and do not turn it over to anyone. When there is an issue, a convener (in the case of schools, typically but not always the principal) announces a meeting and leads a discussion for all those who wish to participate. In this form of democracy, those who attend (or who can attend) decide the priorities, drive further action, and determine the decisionmaking process.

A third and common merger of the two forms of democracy is one that includes a representative council coupled with direct participation in the referendum decisionmaking process. Typically, the representative body is responsible for establishing priorities with informed input from constituents, delegating work to task force groups to make recommendations on possible decisions, and setting timelines for the decisionmaking process. However, all final decisions are made through a direct referendum of the group as a whole. Due to very real time constraints of site-based managed systems, as well as the need to think and act systematically, most high-functioning democratic

Figure 3.1. Representative Form

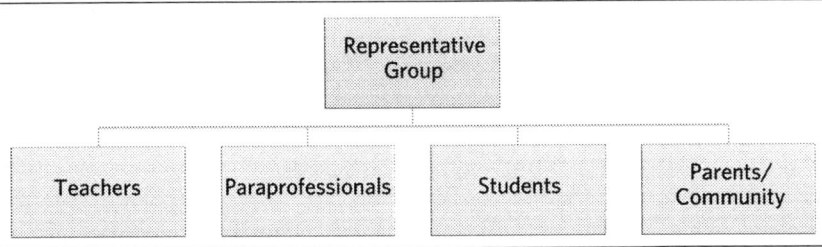

Figure 3.2. Direct Participation

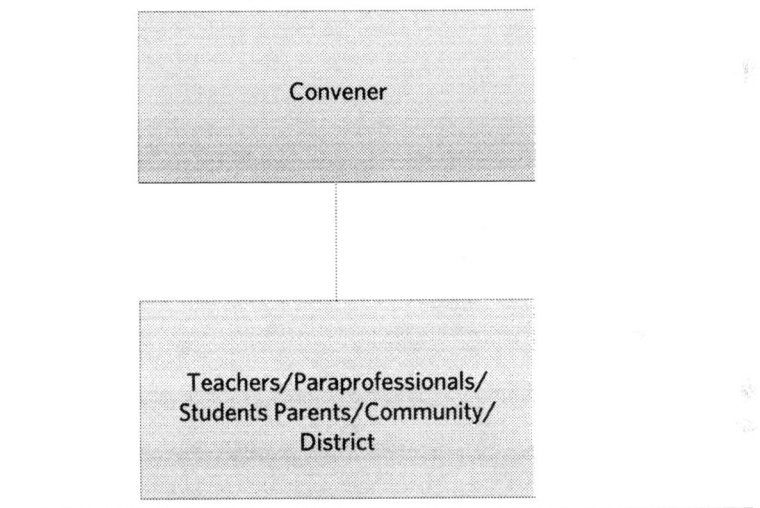

schools develop a hybrid model approach, as represented in Figure 3.3. In this model, once the school council has worked with task force groups, liaisons to various community groups work to receive detailed feedback and communication about recommendations. Afterwards, the school council can either approve the recommendation or bring it back to the body at large for a final vote (see Appendix B for more detail).

WHY DO THIS?

At this point we can imagine teachers, principals, parents, or community members saying, "Why would we need to have this in our schools when we struggle to do all the other things we need to accomplish in a school day?" While it is easy to get lost in the details of the democratization of schools,

Figure 3.3. Hybrid Governance

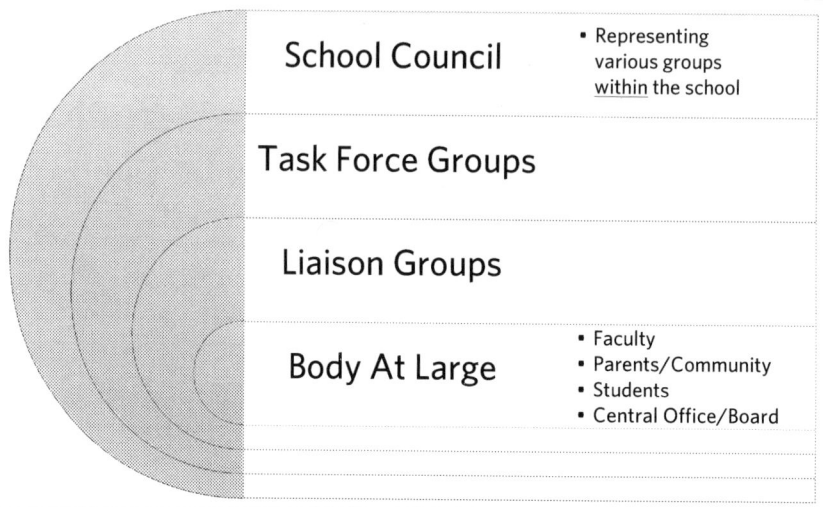

what should not get lost is the spirit of why democracy is crucial to public education. A more democratically governed school allows a local community to focus on what matters *here and now* in our communities, where we have the power and ability to create a more fair and equitable education system through the engagement of students and the families school systems serve.

It is also easy to get lost in the details of democratic governance (although the details are important in the development and acceptance of the school's constitution) and lose the spirit of why being democratically governed is central to and compatible with the purpose of public education. What democratic governance does is strive for decisions that focus on matters of schoolwide education, are fair and equal in distributing power, and are morally consistent with the school's goal of democratic engagement of students.

More often than not, there is a minuscule number of democratic interactions among adults in schools today. Prepackaged curriculum, pacing guides, and predetermined school reform agendas serve to manage schools rather than lead them based on the will of the people they serve. Those reading this will likely nod their head—almost all educators have witnessed administrative-appointed leadership structures that serve to further the interests of those who appointed these departmental and grade-level leaders. We have seen these structures, time and time again, negatively impact adult interactions in schools and challenge the autonomy of trained educators. What we are suggesting is for school systems to use a governing structure with freely elected leadership, whose members are voted on and representative of their respective educational community groups. The sole mission of a democratic governing structure in schools is to create the best education system possible for children based on the commitment to a community. When stakeholders realize that decisions are made in a manner where every vote is equal, where every voice has the opportunity to be heard, and where positions of power are dismantled and reinvested in the wisdom of a collective community, only then will we be able to make the changes necessary from the inside out.

IF NOT US, THEN WHOM?

We openly acknowledge it is much easier to write about disrupting existing organizational patterns for making decisions than it is to actually do so in practice. We are all busy people, with busy schedules, and we have many other responsibilities in our professional and personal lives that might make increasing democracy in education seem difficult or even a waste of time. And yet we are struggling as a country to stay connected and grounded to that which matters most—the communities we live in.

While democracies often seem (and in reality, often are) inefficient, these governing principles were *intended* to be the touchstones of our country based on the conceived idea of governing ourselves rather than being ruled by a tyrant. However, we continue to struggle to see freedom and equality for all Americans, regardless of race, ethnicity, socioeconomic status, gender, or sexual orientation, among many other delineations. American communities simply cannot afford to allow outsiders to make decisions about what is best for local children. Democracy leads to crucial debates, even conflicts, which allow *us* to make decisions for ourselves, not by one or two authority figures. Aside from the moral responsibility of needing to maintain and develop our society, a democratic school is a more satisfying and professionally rewarding place to work, to learn, and to strengthen a community. It is the sharing of power, over time, that leads to true community.

A real frustration for teachers will likely be figuring out how to teach students, keep up with day-to-day classroom responsibilities, and devote time to a schoolwide decisionmaking process. A similar frustration for a principal will be figuring out how to collaboratively establish a governance process; craft a promise that is satisfying to teachers, students, and community members alike; identify priorities for her/his own leadership; and all while keeping up with paperwork, updating teacher supervision and bus schedules, conducting mandatory fire drills, navigating state mandates, and ensuring building maintenance. For parents and community members, a frustration will likely be finding time outside of work to take part in the decisionmaking process. These reasons are real, but they can mask or become excuses for not going forward. Time is always the most valuable resource in any organization, but it should not be an obstacle to moving ahead.

FOCUS ON GOVERNANCE

The question for all members of an educational community should not be "Do we even have time to do this?" but rather "With the time we have, how should we begin this process?" At what level of decisionmaking does a principal feel willing to give up authority and have one vote? At what level of decisionmaking do teachers want to use their available time to be involved? How might the decisionmaking process better include students, parents, and community members more broadly? What decisions should remain mainly administrative? Which ones should simply incorporate a process for input? Which ones are the most important, that all parties would wish to make democratically? This does not have to be an all-or-nothing affair. Instead, it can be a beginning.

The determination of the level and scope of decisions can be done in several ways (see Table 3.1). Faculty, principals, paraprofessionals, parents, and students, independently of each other, should identify areas of schoolwide educational decisions that they would want to be a part of and be willing to share. Another way would be simply to ask, on a survey, that individuals identify the decisions to which they would give the highest priority. Still another way would be to have students, parents, community members, administrators, faculty, and paraprofessionals meet, review data on student progress, and agree on common activities that would represent the first decision areas for democratic governance. In our experiences, and from our perspectives, successful schools are able to develop and approve democratic governance principles and promises that allow them to address community issues in a more direct manner.

A FINAL NOTE ABOUT FORMALITY AND PROCEDURES

To enact a promise for teaching and learning, a school needs a pledge for democratic decisionmaking. Such a pledge must be clearly understood, must communicate the decisionmaking process, and must be approved by those it represents. School systems attempting to become more democratic will need to take into account the history of the school, the community, and the previous process of decisionmaking when considering formal rules and procedures. This means a school community will need to determine whether it will use a majority vote, two-thirds, 80%, or consensus. It also means the school will need to be flexible and update procedures as it implements democratic principles. Once a pledge is developed, it is crucial to implement a trial period of a year, and then allow for policies and procedures to be reviewed and revised. In other words, democratic governing principles have a beginning point, and must be enacted, maintained, reconsidered, and updated—this is the heart of school renewal.

In keeping with the idea that everyone should have the opportunity to participate, be heard, and influence the decisionmaking process, but also balancing the notion that no one is required to participate, school systems need to allow time for democratic principles to flourish. In higher-functioning schools we often see systems use 80% vote of approval, by secret vote of the school community members, in order to ratify and begin. There are schools where an 80% approval process would mean a decision is never made, so a two-thirds vote of the body at large is used to make decisions. Some schools use a simple majority vote, and in some schools, 50% is a major achievement. The point is that the higher the percentage of approval, the greater the chance of commitment. It is a matter of the school system knowing what it is, where it has been, and how it will need to function to move forward. The goal is to begin the democratic process and continually evolve.

All this being said, does a school need a formal constitution and governing organization in order to be democratic? In short, yes, but it needs to be fluid, flexible, and capable of updating to meet the promise and pledge made to a community. Teachers, administrators, students, parents, and community members should work together to establish a clear and formal process that supports a well-defined democratic process with written procedures of two to five pages (see Appendixes B and C for more details). This written document allows everyone to understand the process, identify when procedures are not followed, and make revisions when necessary. In many ways, this process allows schools to transition away from closed systems built on hierarchy and control, and instead build on democratic principles that help address issues within a community. The third part of the structure for school renewal—problem solving via the action research process—gives us the vehicle to drive school and community improvement together.

CHAPTER 4

Problem Solving

Community-Based Action Research to Drive Student Learning

If you visit any number of schools or school districts that have recently received awards and praise for high student achievement and innovation, and you ask teachers and principals to name their school objective, you will likely hear any number of responses. These could include:

- Implementation of curriculum aligned to state standards
- Use of writer's workshop model
- Integration of technology
- Implementation of positive-behavior support system
- Creation of problem-based learning projects
- Formative assessment of student learning
- Increased use of exploratory learning
- Development of dual credit courses
- Implementation of social–emotional curriculum

Many of these schools are considered high achieving or high functioning. And yet none of these innovations directly connect to the objective of a school, per se. Here we see one of the greatest challenges of school renewal, which is the tendency to view school goals and objectives as synonymous with innovations to be implemented. Schools and school districts have been plagued by the perceived pressure to implement innovations since the late 1930s when *The Saber Tooth Curriculum* was published (Benjamin, 1939), highlighting that much of what we teach in schools has little relevance to the lives of students. Sadly, many schools continue with this tradition today—and yet it doesn't need to be this way. If a school chooses an innovation, it should not be simply because it is the next hot thing in an ever-changing list of educational fads. Rather, innovations should be chosen because they meet the needs of students, and the community more broadly.

THE CRITICAL SELF-STUDY PROCESS

When analyzing instructional priorities and innovations as objectives, educators need to ask themselves a few critical questions:

- What effects or results will the innovation have on the students in our school and the parents and community members we serve?
- How is the innovation we hope to implement valued by students?
- Will the innovation have a meaningful, long-lasting impact, or is it a knee-jerk response to something else?

Educators in a school building may have different objectives in mind for how an innovation will be used to address various needs, but what is important is that schools move away from a "keeping up with the Joneses" mentality and focus on what is valued for the purposes of student learning. Goals and objectives for students should be based on the promise that members of the education community make to and for each other. To capture the essence of school renewal, educators need to develop their own problem-solving process that expands the raising and studying of important questions about student learning.

RAISING COMMUNITY-BASED QUESTIONS TO DRIVE ACTION RESEARCH

As we have described up to this point in the book, school renewal and community engagement take time, resources, and human energy. It is worth the cost to improve the results of an educational program—not just with the metric we have become accustomed to in student achievement, but in making our schools more democratic and responsive to local needs. Focusing on community-based needs to improve schools is a foundation to creating better school climates and culture, improving student and parent perceptions, increasing community involvement, and success for students in later schooling. The challenge, however, is to increase the consciousness of all members of a school building (educators, students, parents, and community members) to reflect on what it means to be effective.

A quick check of the pulse of how conscious people are in a local school might be determined with a fairly simple question: "What do you know about our school and how it helps our students?" Listen carefully to the responses and consider the following:

- Do people use clichés or party lines, like "We all work hard here" or "It's a caring place"?

- Are responses supported with statistics, such as "Attendance is up to 92% despite the fact that 65% of our students receive free and reduced lunch" or "We raised proficiency rates by 6% last year when most other districts fell"?
- Are labels used to describe or allude to student achievement, such as "We are a blue-ribbon school" or "We support a lot of students from single-parent households who work multiple jobs"?
- Do people respond about the effectiveness of schools throughout a community based on location, household income, or cultural differences?
- Is the evaluation of a school based on how caring teachers are, based on assessment data generated at the district or state level, determined by athletic dominance through school-based teams, or determined by the "club" status of a particular building as perceived by the community?

These possible responses, and how they vary, tell us a lot about how local stakeholders perceive indicators of success for a school building. They can also provide quite a bit of information based on what is omitted from the responses. From this, schools can consider how information about effectiveness is currently being collected, how (in)complete the data are and where the data are derived from, and how the data inform the educational purposes of a school. This, in turn, can allow educators and stakeholders alike to peel back the onion layers of the educational purposes of a school, specifically revealing how to raise more community-based questions about what data are valued and how the data might be used for setting priorities and determining future actions.

As we have stated previously, for school renewal to be successful, all members of the educational community need to have input to help inform the balcony-level perspective of the overall effectiveness of a building. Using the promise (the common principles of teaching and learning) and the pledge (creating a commitment to make decisions as a community), a school can use community-based action research to problem-solve local issues. It is the use of information from all members of the community that is crucial in supporting critical thinking, data collection, and use of student learning in the community that will determine the success of a school.

DATA SOURCES FOR SELF-STUDY

We believe that now, perhaps more than ever but certainly in the last several generations, the core goal of American PK–12 education should be the preparation of students to be productive members of our society and contributing citizens to our democracy by being empowered to address issues of inequity in their community. The data we collect to inform such an important goal must be different from the data we have insistently been told over the last 15 years we must collect. In Table 4.1 we offer some examples of data use in schools, and some examples schools might consider using. Data are classified according to sources. *Accountability sources* are those we have been told we must collect, are often tied to funding, and traditionally are quantitative data. *Progressive sources* come from data that can be collected and analyzed with some additional effort, and typically are qualitative in nature. *Creative sources* are typically project based, expressive, and possibly relayed in the form of a performance.

Every school has access to reports, files, and accountability data sources compiled by the district, state, or federal government. These schoolwide accountability data sources we are all familiar with—assessment scores, attendance rates, course grades, discipline referrals, number of dropouts, the number of students retained, and special education markers, among others. The compilation of accountability data, as originally designed, was *intended* to help make comparisons across a large district or a state in order to review the data and determine how to pursue improvements. Especially in a democratic school, accountability data can and should be used appropriately to raise certain issues, such as gender, racial and ethnic, and socioeconomic equality.

However, democratic schools are much more than a collection of numbers. Some schools have begun collecting more progressive data sources, many of which are qualitatively descriptive. The progressive

Table 4.1. Data Sources

Accountability	Progressive	Creative
Assessment scores	Student portfolios	Student exhibits
Attendance rates	Student and parent surveys	Community-based activities within the school
Course grades	Project-based learning	Podcasts, videos, and multimedia production shared through social media
Discipline referrals	Restorative practices	Community-based learning projects
Dropout rates	Alternative education programs	Individualized learning for all students
Retention rates	Proficiency-based learning	
Special education progress	Developmental progress beyond academic measures	

data sources provide evidence of a shift away from traditional PK–12 paradigms of what education either should be or has been. The use of student and parent surveys, including written comments that are coded for themes, provides more of a 360° approach to feedback on student achievement and student learning more broadly. Project-based learning helps detail learning in action and results in end products that can be used in the school or community. Restorative practices go beyond the reporting, or implementation, of discipline and attempt to address the root cause of the behavior, which often originates with an issue at home or in the community. Alternative education programs provide students who are at risk with alternative pathways to earning a high school diploma. Proficiency-based instruction can be used schoolwide or on an individualized basis, the latter often helping prevent retaining students who struggle at a set point in time or grade level. And there are important developmental progress reports that go beyond traditional academic measures that can be used to show student growth. All of these allow for the collection of progressive data sources, often through interviews that indicate how school experiences can and should go beyond simply using accountability measures to determine the success of a school.

Creative data sources are examples of what schools *can be*; however, most schools do not typically focus on activities that generate these types of data. Examples of creative data sources include student exhibits, such as products and projects that require imaginative application of knowledge. Community-based activities held within the school are an alternative measure to show correlations between parent/guardian attendance and targeted efforts to increase chronically absent students. End-of-course products, such as podcasts, videos, or other multimedia productions that are shared through social media to inform the public of students work, can complement or replace course grades. Community-based learning projects, work that targets the source of community issues, can be used as evidence for reduced discipline referrals. And, broadly speaking, the more individualized learning that occurs for all students, the less likely we are to see high dropout rates and high retention rates, and the more likely we are to see success for all students, regardless of diagnosis.

In order to produce more progressive and creative data sources, we have to be willing to ask ourselves some tough questions about traditional education that has been reinforced with accountability data. For example, why might only a few students feel comfortable presenting in front of an entire class? Why can many students verbalize critical-thinking skills but poorly apply them on a written test? How can most students use ethical reasoning in a simulation to determine that robbery is wrong, and yet their behavior in school fails to apply this ethical reasoning and they accept or ignore theft? These are the types of questions we need to ask ourselves as we reimagine our democracy.

AN AMERICAN TENDENCY: ACTION WITHOUT STUDY

In America we have a tendency to direct our attention to the activities of what *others* do rather than reflecting on what we need to do in our own school. It is only after we study ourselves that we should take action, and if we act without studying, we often make little to no progress and spend quite a bit of money in the process. Additionally, when we do this, we deplete goodwill among our faculty and staff, eventually causing people to say, "This too shall pass." Studying and acting, in an interrelated process, leads to a more educated, purposeful school system.

There are some caveats to the problem-solving process that schools may find useful. First, we need to begin by looking at existing data and decide what other types of data are needed to better evaluate our own school. Second, we need to determine how to study our own actions and predetermine how we will measure success with our actions. Third, we should try to identify and use existing resources within a school and the community to promote a "work smarter, not harder" approach to data collection and interpretation. Fourth, we should try to create synergy between the improvement work occurring *within* a school and those occurring *outside* the school.

A generic outline to develop a community-based action research plan includes the criteria found in Figure 4.1. Based on the work done in creating the promise and the pledge, educators can begin to work together to problem-solve and address issues facing the school and community more broadly. During this process, educators should reflect on the goals that are considered critical to the self-study. Through this work, they can identify baseline data that needs to be collected, how new information will be collected and analyzed, and how the interpretation of the data will inform actions, activities, and eventually new goals.

We should point out that this process *values* data, and that we believe data are critical to understanding the health and vitality of a school. However, we believe that data must be used for democratic governance, which moves away from strict accountability standards and instead provides a local school degrees of freedom to determine how it will use data

Figure 4.1. Community-Based Action Research Plan

Section 1	Goal(s)
Section 2	Student objectives
Section 3	Activities to accomplish objectives
Section 4	Evaluation of student results (outcomes)
Section 5	Resources needed

(It is useful for plans to be specific in detailing *who* will be responsible for *what*, *when*, and *how*).

to compare outcomes (McDonald, 2019). Educators reading this book understand wiggle room is needed for local schools to address areas of need based on their own neighborhood or community they serve, and that for school renewal to occur, we must empower them to take discretionary action to improve outcomes for students. This is the truest form of accountability, and as we detail in the next section, accountability can only occur when a school is allowed to take part in action research, identify successes and opportunities for improvement, and share these lessons with the community.

INFUSION OF INFORMATION

The problem-solving process is, essentially, an internal accountability system. It determines how to assess the needs of students, creates goals and objectives, and then implements action plans that are eventually assessed for results. What is just as important, however, is how information is gathered from outside the knowledge base of the school building and community partners. Just like we need to honor the voices of members of a community, we also need to seek out information from other educational organizations that have attempted to address problems of practice, specifically what has been implemented and learned in other laboratories of practice. To attempt to make decisions about school improvement and renewal without learning from others hurts education as a profession. Just like medical doctors read journals to help improve their own practice, so can educators act as scholarly practitioners. As a profession, it is important for education to use information and different points of view to develop a critical stance about instruction and student learning.

Thus, a school, which is the institutional foundation to preparing students to live within a democracy, needs to model how it collects information from a variety of sources to then make an independent decision. In a time and climate of "fake news," this has never been more important. Before a school makes a decision about change (e.g., curriculum, schedule, staff development, student grouping, etc.), it must first seek out information from professional journals, professional conferences, visitations to other schools, or graduate courses, just to name a few. This can then lead to faculty discussions or book clubs, as well as interacting with a wide variety of videos found on the Internet, social media accounts, or podcasts created to address the issue at hand. As we are now perhaps in the (dis)information age, never has it been more important to function as scholarly practitioners who are able to digest information and work collaboratively to make informed decisions that will help revive a school and the community it serves. Together, as a group, members of a school community need to be responsible to one another to be informed and to help make informed decisions.

Knowledge is a form of power. Think about all the prepackaged curricula that are sold to schools and school districts every year—the knowledge held in the prepackaged curriculum translates into economic power for the education industry and is supported by political power that says schools must meet certain state or federal guidelines. However, power lies within each individual in a democracy as well. Educators have the power to access knowledge from various sources and use this knowledge to renew education within our schools, but we must take the time to make our own informed decisions about how our schools will function.

We know how busy PK–12 educators are with day-to-day routines, and we acknowledge that professional organizations and education systems could do a better job of working together to bridge the theory–practice gap. The American Educational Research Association has an annual conference where literally tens of thousands of research papers are presented. Hundreds of books on education are printed each year by various publishing houses. And yet very few of these important resources translate into discussions within the walls of school buildings.

WAYS TO GATHER INFORMATION

If we are to renew America's PK–12 public school system, we must make knowledge acquisition a priority and not simply a matter of chance. Systematically, schools must develop plans for accessing and retrieving information. Perhaps just as importantly, we must be able to develop our own knowledge through action research in order to tailor our specific professional needs. In other words, instructional goals and objectives must go beyond hopping on the next bandwagon. Instead, we must look at school renewal as an internal process, one where we study ourselves, the organization, and our community. Using the promise and pledge, we can problem-solve anything that is preventing a school from producing productive citizens in our democracy. If a school discovers there is a lack of student voice in learning, the school should seek information at a conference to see how other schools have increased students' voice. If a self-study determines a lack of culturally relevant pedagogy, the school should read articles and visit other schools that address this issue. If the data suggest a disconnect from the learning that is valued at school compared to home, the school should create an ad hoc committee of teachers and students to learn more about the issue firsthand. With this additional information, from journals, conferences, online material, observations of other practices, and perceptions within a community, schools are empowered to understand more fully what can be done to address students' needs.

As discussed previously in this chapter, information can be gathered in multiple ways. Table 4.2 highlights some of these outlets of professional

Table 4.2. Outlets of Professional Learning

Sources of learning	Learning outcomes
Journal articles	Synthesized research; case study examples of improvement actions
On-site visits to other schools	Comparable communities; anecdotal information on problems of practice
Professional conferences	Presentations from policymakers, researchers, and other practitioners
Graduate courses	Classes that address the intersection of theory and practice
Books	Concepts and ideas about school improvement
Social media	Practitioner-friendly accounts highlighting best practices
Community members	Local ideas about how knowledge is applied in a community

learning, which should be used as sources of information to drive conversations about school renewal. On a small scale, this can occur in grade-level teams or within departments. On a slightly larger scale, it can occur across teams within a school building. On an even larger scale, it can occur across buildings within a school district, or at the regional or state level. The point is, teams of teachers can and should be part of learning communities that bring in new ideas, share information from their own action research, and actively contribute to school renewal more broadly.

In discussing ways to infuse knowledge and information into schools, particularly how to problem-solve through action research, we run the risk of insulting educators who are part of learning organizations that do this work on a daily basis. Nonetheless, it is our experience that schools are often isolated from information other than that which is provided by their own school or school district. As schools have progressed through the last decade and a half, teachers have become busier and more burdened with requirements imposed *on them* rather than *having a say* in the data collection efforts to help improve their school. If we are to increase democracy in our public PK–12 school system, we must reinvest in our own professional learning and systematically gather information about how to improve instruction at the local level. Far too often we legitimize the consulting and writing of people who are too far removed from the day-to-day practice of practitioners in schools. Instead of spending large sums of money to attend one-day professional development trainings that never translate into better practices in schools, we need to value the voices of scholarly practitioners who highlight exemplary practices at the local, regional, state, and national level. It is the strength of information carried and passed between credible practitioners that is often ignored, and we must work to empower these types of exchanges.

GIVING VOICE

To learn what is needed in a school, we must be willing to give voice—a voice to ourselves, to each other, to students, and to our community. When we give voice, we acknowledge the wisdom that lives inside us all, and it reinforces the belief that we have the answers to our problems inside of us already, not from a prepackaged curriculum or a high-priced professional development speaker. Voice comes from ideas that are heard, explored, considered, discussed, planned, implemented, studied, and examined. Most importantly, voice comes from multiple perspectives, and it is not one voice that constantly adds her or his own opinion that matters, but rather the collective voice that is powerful.

When schools give voice to those whose voice has historically been suppressed, education expands the knowledge base of the entire school. It takes courage and dedication to find your voice, to empower others to no longer relinquish their voice, but once this happens, a school will never be the same. Giving voice can come in the form of a task force that examines discipline practices that disproportionately suspend minority children. It can come in the form of a book club that studies discriminatory policies and practices against students transitioning to another gender. It can be fueled by visiting another school building with identical demographics and noticing a completely different and more positive culture among teachers. It can especially be powerful when community members are asked their opinion, are brought into the school to share their personal stories, and help address the disconnect between school and home. Problem solving through community-based action research not only gives voice to the voiceless, it also models how to increase democracy in schools.

Part II

THE WORK OF SCHOOL RENEWAL

CHAPTER 5

Educational Priorities and Organizational Application

School renewal is brought about through the three-dimensional approach we have described up to this point in the book. Figure 5.1 illustrates these concepts, and in this chapter, we discuss in more detail how they can be used to determine educational priorities and be applied directly to schools. The promise—establishing common principles of teaching and learning—helps give the school continuity in its educational purpose. The pledge—creating a commitment to make decisions as a community—provides the framework to govern a school democratically when making schoolwide educational decisions. And the problem-solving process—using community-based action research to drive student learning—provides a system-thinking approach to analyzing instructional and student needs to help improve student outcomes.

The work of school renewal is a self-driven process, one where local schools and the communities they serve work together using the three-dimensional framework to address the ultimate form of accountability: preparing students to become productive and contributing citizens to our society. The educational priorities of a school—the topics that educators can focus on to help prepare students to engage in our democracy—help strengthen instructional outcomes for students. These priorities include 1) curriculum development and implementation, 2) staff professional development, 3) instructional coaching, 4) student assessment and outcomes, and 5) instructional resources.

The following provides descriptions for educators to consider, as well as questions to be asked, in order to help bridge the gap between current instructional practices and the school's promise to achieve common principles of teaching and learning. The intent is to empower educators to prioritize what is important for instructional practices, and to continually work toward a collegial educational organization. When considering these priorities, we describe them as mutually exclusive items, but in application they are inherently intertwined.

Figure 5.1. School Renewal Framework

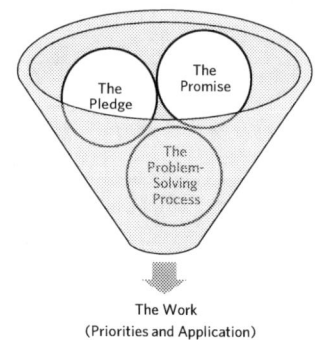

The Work
(Priorities and Application)

CURRICULUM DEVELOPMENT AND IMPLEMENTATION

The curriculum a school or school district chooses is essentially a program of study for students. When evaluating curricula, education systems need to consider if what is being studied is mainly a vestige of the past or if it is helping students be better educated and prepared for the future. Curricula *should* correspond to current social and community issues, which in turn helps students to be critical consumers of knowledge and information. In doing so, the hope is to develop self-reliant citizens who are confident in their abilities to deal with personal matters and broader societal concerns.

Some basic considerations of what the curriculum is can be addressed by the content and objectives covered, the order of subjects and developmental themes taught, and the emphasis placed on certain forms of learning and student outcomes expected. However, additional considerations and questions should be asked as well, including:

- Does the existing curriculum correspond to *how* students learn and what they *should* learn?
- Is the curriculum consistent with the value of preparing students for productive citizenship in a democratic society?
- Does the curriculum reflect culturally relevant topics, or is diversity represented through perpetuation of stereotypes, and token events or celebrations?
- Does what students learn have real applications, allowing them to making connections of knowledge to life outside of school?
- Do students have an active, ongoing voice in what they learn?
- How is curriculum determined, and is there an overall school curriculum, or does it reflect individual departments, grade levels, or subject areas?

- Does the curriculum reflect the concerns and values of the community, and do parents and community members have a chance to be involved?

Another consideration, as well as a set of questions to consider, has to do with the implementation of prepackaged curriculum programs that are created as part of the American PK–12 industry. Veteran teachers likely remember the time when educators were responsible for generating their own thoughts and ideas on how to best develop a curriculum for students. Currently, however, many different kinds of curricula are determined at the state and federal level, and then developed by corporations with fairly tight alignment to state standardized tests. Even nonacademic curricula, such as positive behavior support systems, restorative justice structures, and social–emotional programs, are prepackaged and sold to school systems looking to address a need in their community.

While externally constructed, field-tested prepackaged curricula have their place and value, many are overly simplistic, commercialized, and marketed with the belief that local practitioners are unable to identify solutions to their own problems. There are some important questions school organizations should ponder when considering buying and implementing a prepackaged curriculum:

- How prescriptive is the curriculum, and does it give suggestions on how to adapt it to meet the individualized needs of communities?
- How controlled is the use of textbooks, workbooks, and assessments, or is there flexibility for faculty to modify sequencing and use their own materials?
- How well does the prepackaged curriculum fit with the priorities established by the school, particularly as it relates to the compatibility of the promise and the principles of teaching and learning?
- What research is available to support the implementation of a prepackaged curriculum and whether such a program is worth implementing or continuing?
- What training and ongoing professional development are needed to support the use of textbooks, instructional materials, and differentiated teaching strategies?

Curriculum development and implementation, as well as the review of curriculum, are perhaps one of the most important priorities for a school organization to consider in the school renewal process. These considerations reflect a shift toward accountability to a community, rather than a standardized test, and focus on developing responsible citizens who will be capable of contributing to a democracy. Key to this process is considering how time and money used for curriculum development and implementation purposes reflect a commitment to the community and local expertise more generally. If there is a lack of fit with the curriculum and the priorities of the community, a change should be made.

STAFF PROFESSIONAL DEVELOPMENT

In order to provide structured activities that will support the development of staff's knowledge and skills, schools typically provide professional development opportunities. These activities can be stipulated, paid, or otherwise required by the school organization and come in various forms and modes of delivery. Generally speaking, the most common come in the form of school-based professional development that involve early-release days and/or the full professional development in-service days that are built into the school calendar (before the start of the school year, during the school year, and after the end of the school year). Other forms of staff professional development include attending workshops, professional conferences, or professional classes devoted to learning activities that are intended to be implemented directly into practice. (We do not define staff development as including educational activities pursued by educators on their own time and at their own expense, such as graduate programs, attendance at their own professional association meetings, and educational trips to other countries. However, pipeline development programs paid for by a school district intended to directly impact practices in a school system would qualify.)

When considering what a faculty needs to learn in order to improve, refine, or reimagine teaching practices across the entire school and become more consistent with the promise for teaching and learning, we provide some questions below to consider.

- How does a school reflect on the variety of teaching techniques and pedagogy (lecture, repetition, student-to-student conversations, or creation/evaluation) used throughout a school building?
- How should a school ensure that all teachers learn how to make more intensive use of technology in the classroom?
- How should students' experiences with technology inform the application of technology in the classroom?
- How do faculty members use a common form of positive behavior management?
- Should teachers know how to use mastery learning techniques, cooperative learning, critical-thinking strategies, constructivist approaches, and project-based and community-centered learning activities?

These questions should not only help the school organization function better, but should also help teachers with individualized professional development. Most districts provide districtwide required professional development; however, many struggle to provide individualized opportunities. Perhaps of greatest importance is the need to build in opportunities for teachers to share what they have learned in their professional development, and to apply it directly in their everyday practice.

INSTRUCTIONAL COACHING

Receiving feedback and coaching on instructional methods is a formative (nonevaluative) process that is intended to help develop a reflective stance about instruction. It is a nonhierarchical process that values the relationship between the teacher and the educator providing feedback (whether that is a peer, an instructional coach, or an administrator). Specifically, instructional coaching is personalized feedback provided to a teacher based on firsthand observations that teachers use to think more deeply about pedagogy and instructional methods.

Instructional coaching is crucial to the school renewal process in terms of the educational priorities of developing common teaching and learning principles within a school building. With no feedback or discussion from others, it is difficult for an individual teacher to know how consistent his or her teaching is with the school promise, or how to become more consistent with it. Leaving people alone to do the best they can sends a quiet but clear message: The school is not really serious about teachers' learning from one another and becoming a school community. Instead, often schools continue the tradition of operating in silos and protecting the privacy of teachers.

However, there are some questions that can be asked when considering school renewal, specifically about the de-privatization of teaching and the impact this can have on bettering instruction. The following questions incorporate some important concepts:

- How often do teachers have people (administrators and other teachers) come into their classrooms for extended periods to observe the principles of learning that the teachers are striving to implement?
- Do these observations include discussions to help guide teachers' further planning?
- How aware are teachers of one another's teaching?
- Is there a system of peer coaching that allows for the release of faculty to visit with one another and focus on particular schoolwide teaching purposes?

- Are such visits reciprocal and collaborative (peer coaching), rather than remedial and hierarchical (mentor-mentee or master teacher–lead teacher relationships)?
- How clearly is it understood that these visits, observations, and discussions, regardless of who initiates them, are for purposes of assistance, rather than for ranking and evaluation?

More refined questions about coaching have to do with who visits whom. For a school to be a community, its members need to be aware of the entire school. Peer coaching that goes on primarily within grade levels, teams, or departments reinforces the idea that the school is mainly a physical space for the particular groups. Instead, faculty need to spend time observing and discussing teaching with teachers at other grade levels, in other departments, on other teams, and in other physical places within the school. This arrangement gives each faculty member a better sense of the entire school. There can also be a role for parents and community members to assist a school in its coaching process, and students can visit other classrooms to find connections across seemingly disparate grade levels and courses.

STUDENT ASSESSMENT AND OUTCOMES

The various ways of assessing student learning must also be examined in order to improve teaching and learning as part of the school renewal process. A truism we have come to accept in education is that teachers teach what students are tested on. However, there is a growing shift in opinion on what matters as the end product as a student finishes a grade level or graduates from a school system. Schools that believe standardized tests are the best measures of student learning arrange their classrooms and use instructional time and teaching techniques differently from the schools that believe students' actual performance or learning outcome is the more important measure of learning. In the former case, classrooms are organized for students to learn sequences of skills and knowledge in a more directive, teacher-centered manner. In the latter case, students have more open-ended opportunities in classroom activities and discussions to explore how to apply the knowledge in context.

Schools need to take a close look not only at how they assess individual students but also at what they expect in terms of student outcomes. How schools use individual assessments, and how they report such assessment to students and parents, is important as it relates to high-stakes standardized tests. However, the ability to creatively apply the knowledge to a local context is what schools are ultimately responsible for achieving in a democratic society. A simple example could come in the form of a student-led project, initiative, or activity that empowers student voice and allows students to apply learned concepts to real-world social concerns that are experienced within a community. Another, more complex example of this might be a high school that requires a yearlong performance exhibition that integrates communication, physical representation, and a written scientific rationale as a graduation requirement, which forces the curriculum, instructional programs, and staff development across departments to be more reflective of such an integrative assessment and outcome.

Determining how students will be assessed, and the outcomes they are expected to produce, can be a highly creative space for educators to consider as an educational priority. Aspects to reflect on entail:

- Are the school's current testing and assessment practices consistent with the promise?
- Are there glaring gaps between what the school claims to believe about learning and what it assesses?
- Is how student learning is recorded (report cards, progress reports) consistent with expected outcomes?
- Are the results of student learning assessments and outcomes used to inform actions within the community?
- How can parents, other community members, and students become more involved in the development and implementation of new assessment procedures and development of new outcomes?
- Is assessment related to the application of knowledge and skills in a real-world setting?

Assessment has continually been seen as a crucial issue in public education. However, there has been increasing questioning among parents, communities, school districts, and even state departments of education about the value of using standardized student assessments for assessing school quality (Hess & McShane, 2019). This issue, as well as most others in this book, will not be resolved overnight and will have to be worked on one step at a time. What is most auspicious in this new questioning of traditional assessment practices is that schools, through a democratic governance process, may have the opportunity to develop, within their communities, measures of student outcomes of the greatest worth that are consistent with their agreed-upon promises. Thus, they will be able to demonstrate that the learning of greatest worth is being achieved.

INSTRUCTIONAL RESOURCES

Very few people or organizations have the money that they desire or need, but the existing money can still be a resource in a school that has control over the budget and pays for staff positions, teaching materials, and staff development time. Traditionally, most of the instructional budget has been used to support normal school operations. Each year, the same amounts are spent in basically the same ways, to do the same things (replacing teachers, adopting new textbooks and testing forms and scoring services, and setting aside planning days). With more money, a school can surely do more for its students, but the first two pragmatic questions are "With our existing money, are we doing the right thing?" and "With more money, would we be doing more of the right things?"

Beyond the questions and beliefs about the use of money is the need to consider resources more broadly. In reimagining the use of resources, specifically human resources, school renewal can be applied in bold new ways to fuel the school promise and address the school's teaching and learning priorities. Useful questions might include:

- Rather than being divided among various "fiefdoms" within the school, how might money, human resources, and intellectual value be reconsidered to address community needs or concerns?
- Why spend money on textbooks or consumable workbooks if other learning materials or human resources can be redirected to be more relevant to the learning principles?
- Why divide resources by department and grade level if the school is striving for schoolwide goals?
- Why not look at the instructional budget and pool of resources as a flexible application of tools to address school priorities that meets the needs of the community to gain additional power?

We acknowledge that money can be a sensitive issue for many district officials and school administrators, particularly for those who want to "play" the budget "close to the vest" to have room to respond to special needs or emergencies. That being said, democratizing school systems will only work well for all members of the community, particularly community groups that have been historically underrepresented, when school systems openly debate and decide how to collectively best use their resources. In communities and school systems where individuals keep public funds hidden, subsections of people depend on the individual authority that holds the purse for use of resources, which can trigger distrust and encourage potential abuse and unethical conduct. Locally dedicated schools do not need to keep faculty, staff members, or other community members ignorant when it comes to how resources are used or applied. If a democracy is real, then part of its reality is its resources. For the school community to decide what it wants for students is the first step. The second step is to openly discuss how to allocate its resources accordingly.

IMPLEMENTING NEW PRACTICES

It is one thing to know about all these priorities; however, it can be much more difficult to decide how to implement and apply these concepts to an educational organization. However, decades of research on educational innovations, whatever their nature, have shown that what a school community learns and sustains, in terms of new ways of teaching and new ways of student learning, often can be structured through a three-phase sequence (Fahey, Breidenstein, Ippolito, & Hensley, 2019; Meier & Gasoi, 2017). Essentially, educators wanting to increase democracy in a school system need to a) cognitively explore, b) apply in practice, and c) interpersonally reflect on how priorities impact teaching and learning outcomes.

First, new approaches to teaching and learning must be cognitively digested and explained. Faculty members need to be allowed to wrestle with what the approach is about, what it purports to do, what it consists of, and what the results have been to contextualize their own understanding. It is then necessary to see what it looks like, how the materials are used, what teaching methods are employed, what technology is employed, how students are organized, and how classrooms are to be physically arranged to maximize the priorities and purposes of education.

Second, the faculty needs opportunities for applied practice, and—of equal importance—for nonjudgmental feedback to help continually improve teaching and learning. Once a faculty is able to experiment with how various approaches work, the internalization process begins. Teachers can see value to the new approaches with other teachers in workshops, under the guidance of a person with expertise in those approaches or based on group decisions about how to assess implementation. As faculty members continue to apply new concepts to their own classrooms, skills are sharpened with the support from other colleagues who also are piloting the change and are able to observe and give formative feedback to one another.

Third, implementation is sustained by having faculty members involved in ongoing meetings, where they interpersonally reflect, brainstorm, and revise the use of the new approaches. Once teachers have piloted the new approaches and received feedback from colleagues or experts, they will be more likely to change their previous routines and adopt the new approaches. Implementation can be maintained if the faculty has continual opportunities to discuss and share successes, failures, and ongoing concerns. In such settings, colleagues help refine one another's skills, find new adaptations, and keep the focus on change until the change becomes a normal operation within the school.

It is important to note that stakeholders in the school community need to be involved and to see an innovation as part of their school's overall direction. According to participants' concerns, there may be a need to give greater emphasis to a particular phase of this three-stage sequence. It takes extended practice and application before a particular change becomes routinized. After that, however, conceptual distinctions among previous educational tasks disappear over the long term as implementation of new schoolwide approaches to teaching and learning take hold.

STAGES OF CONCERN

Ideas for change in teaching and learning priorities should come from the people who will be affected. To truly democratize a school system, approaches are best developed from the promise and the pledge so that the application of proposed changes come from those who govern themselves. When this happens, the old problem of resistance to externally imposed ideas about school reform should become less of an issue. The larger issue becomes one of degree of emphasis, as well as the pacing of change. Those who have studied the change literature have noted that the demise of many reforms has been due to a failure to account for the specific stages of participants' concerns (Breidenstein, Fahey, Glickman, & Hensley, 2012; Glickman, Gordon, & Ross-Gordon, 2018).

We believe there is a useful framework about the stages of concern that educators should consider as they plan for addressing instructional priorities. These stages align directly to the implementation of new practices that we described in the previous section. As detailed in Figure 5.2, these stages include orientation, integration, and refinement, and are illuminated by the major questions that participants have about particular instructional changes.

As educators cognitively explore new ways of thinking about teaching and learning, success will be more likely to occur if there is an orientation structure to help support the change. Often, educators will find themselves

Figure 5.2. Matching Implementation with Concerns

Cognitive Exploration
- Orientation (Why should I do this?)

Application in Practice
- Integration (How do I apply this in my classroom?)

Interpersonal Reflection
- Refinement (How can we better learn together?)

asking an important central question, "Why should I do this?" As teachers and administrators work toward applying the new concepts in practice, an integration framework will be helpful. A typical question in this phase might be, "How do I apply this in my classroom?" or "What resources and support are available to help me apply this in my classroom?" Perhaps most importantly, as groups of teachers take part in interpersonal reflection, a refinement paradigm can support change and school renewal. A useful question to help refine practice could be, "How can we better learn together?" or even "How can we work more cohesively as a group of educators to improve our instructional practices?" Even if all, or nearly all, educators have agreed to the change, the various levels of concern may be different, and as a result implementation may fail if planning is not sensitive to these differences.

Those at the orientation stage need explanation and demonstration, so that they can understand the benefits and see how others like themselves have used the new approach in their classrooms. Those at the integration stage need more trial and practice, role-playing, classroom practice, and feedback from others. Those at the refinement stage need more time for exploring and troubleshooting with other users through group brainstorming and problem solving. Mismatching stages of concern with phases of implementation may ensure failure, while matching the stages and phases can help guide the pace and emphasis of school change. If nothing more, being metacognitive of these different phases is crucial in considering where a school is (and what resources are needed) in the school renewal process.

Of course, educators do not fall neatly into stages of concern, nor does implementation fall into a clean, invariable sequence of phases. In most schools, teachers have multiple levels of concern with educational approaches. Nevertheless, these stages and phases can give further understanding of the complexities of school change and, when accounted for, can help give schools criteria for determining overall plans. Once the people associated with a school have decided to harness their resources according to school priorities and plans, they must work together to make the planned educational change a reality.

BLURRING OF TASKS

Educational tasks are the enabling activities that accomplish school priorities. In practice the tasks should not stand separately. This is where schools can lose energy and direction. Curriculum development and implementation should coincide with staff professional development. Instructional coaching should reinforce curriculum and staff development. Student assessment and outcomes should reflect corresponding changes in curriculum. The instructional resources provided should supporting the priorities and applications needed to change the school system. When each task is seen as a project unto itself, with its own goals, activities, and budget, a school merely has a set of "projects" going on, with no articulation of its promise.

Many highly innovative schools have no links and do not know where they are going. In an individual school, one can find the curriculum being changed to reflect scientific literacy across disciplines, while staff professional development is tangentially connected to the latest educational fad. Conversely, in a successful democratic school, educators perform tasks quite differently. Consider the schoolwide learning objective of a middle school: to have students understand the various forms of mass communication and know how to use various forms of media to participate in issues of the local community. Developing such an objective is relatively easy; planning to attain it is hard. A school attains this goal by examining its educational priorities, developing activities, and aligning its human and financial resources. Answers to the following questions help integrate those tasks:

1. How do we need to change our curriculum across the school to reflect this new emphasis?
2. What staff professional development will be essential for faculty?
3. What instructional coaching will be necessary to give feedback to teachers in implementing the curriculum and the new teaching strategies?
4. What type of support, materials, training, and internal development would it be useful to incorporate into the changes in curriculum, staff development, and coaching?
5. What changes have to be made in how we assess student learning, and what are the outcomes we hope to measure?
6. How much money and time should we allocate, and what resources from the community can we secure, for attainment of this objective?

DEPARTMENTAL AND GRADE-LEVEL PLANS

Not every learning objective needs an individual written plan. Most schools will have many learning objectives, and a single plan that shows how they all can be accomplished is appropriate. Furthermore, a school needs to avoid spending so much time on planning that it never gets around to taking action. Action, planning, and study should be simultaneous; one activity should feed information into the others.

Schoolwide emphasis may sound fine, but aren't there different groups, with their own alignments and distinct purposes? Will they surrender their purposes to the common good? In the ordinary world of schools, the focus is on subgroups. In high schools, departments stick together and have their own budgets and planning meetings. In the middle school, departmental or, more often, grade-level teams and specialists work together. In the elementary school, grade- and age-level groups work together. Nothing in our discussion so far contradicts the reality that subgroups do work together to attain schoolwide goals. The individual subgroups of a school, as long as the school is organized that way, will continue to have some of their own curricula, staff development, coaching, instructional programs, assessment, and instructional budgets. But subgroups' plans can be developed as semi-autonomous parts of the overarching promise and pledge. They become individual patches of the quilt. They are not the quilt itself.

Subgroups will always exist, but what makes a school powerful and purposeful is not what is done only in isolation but what is done together. Emily Gasoi (Meier & Gasoi, 2017) is a teacher who had moved from a traditional public school marked by isolation and conformity and joined a school that began to create a special place for all. She wrote, "We strove to cultivate . . . 'hungry students'—those who are genuinely interested in making sense of the world . . . not afraid to tinker, to question, to wrestle with open ended questions, to get wrong answers, and to make mistakes. These were the skills that we, as teachers, modeling democratic values, felt we needed." And this notion is at the very heart of school renewal for educators who want to rethink the educational priorities of their organization.

CHAPTER 6

Becoming an Educative Community

If you have read up to this point, you might think to yourself, "This seems pretty straightforward. We can use this three-dimensional approach in my school to help provide a framework for school improvement. Nothing to it, right?"

While we would agree that the framework provided in this book will help your school function as a more democratic organization, there are some important realities to consider when implementing change. These include, but are not limited to, embedded cultural norms and expectations, power and politics around school leadership positions, and the real struggle to transition from identifying an inequity to addressing it in action. This chapter and the next provide guidance for how to enter into school renewal at the school building level. The remaining chapters address the important role of support at the district level, as well as the collaboration necessary from the school board and the teachers' union, in order to help inform and provide feedback for policymakers developing school reform at the state and federal level.

CHANGE AND THE SHADOWS OF OUR OWN CAVES

For those familiar with Plato's *The Republic*, and more specifically the telling of the parable of the cave, there is an important lesson to consider when renewing our schools. In the parable of the cave, Plato shares a simple but reflective story about a group of cave dwellers who mistake the shadows that are cast against their cave wall for reality, eliciting fear of the shadows (as well as the source causing the shadows) and highlighting the belief that it is safer to stay in the cave than it is to venture outside of it (Hutchens, 1999). Their images and assumptions about reality, influenced by misinformation and fears, occur in modern-day organizations as well. All across America people in organizational lives struggle to distinguish the difference between shadows cast against a wall and reality. This is especially true in educational organizations attempting to adopt school renewal.

In order to move past shadowy images and fear of change, a school community must help each other change mental models about how a school can (and should) function. This takes time, support, and perhaps of most importance, the willingness to live with discomfort when going through the change process. It is the ability to accept discomfort that allows schools to move past the obstacle of inequities that exist in our school buildings and address them in action. In fact, disrupting existing mental models about "what schools are" is the heart of school renewal.

Educators who work in a democratic school system that is self-renewing understand that at any point in time something might disrupt the clean and orderly system we have expected schools to become the last several decades. However, we know school systems do not function in this manner, as schools are merely a reflection of our American society that is constantly in flux (Morgan, 2006). Over time, schools that acknowledge the challenge of maintaining democratic ideals and beliefs will be better equipped to address crises, defuse issues, resolve problems, and support their community in developing productive citizens than schools that maintain the mental model of schools as a collection of inputs and outputs that produce widgets. However, it takes time and dedication to change mental models and make decisions that are based on democratic ideas and adhere to the promise, pledge, and problem-solving process around community-based school renewal. Inevitably, change is difficult and will be challenged by naysayers who are fearful of their own shadows and who benefit from schools maintaining a hierarchical system. Educators will have to deal with these naysayers, but they can also help others move past their fears about change and create new mental models about what a school can mean to a community revitalization.

UNDERSTANDING (DE)MOTIVATING FACTORS: APPROACHES TO SCHOOL CHANGE

How does a school community know what it is ready to take on in the change process? How might individuals understand more of what they are ready to do? In what ways can a school be mobilized as a community and still respect individual and group differences? These are not always easy questions to answer, but they are critical to consider. In order to help analyze these approaches to change, it is important to consider various approaches to leadership, adult learning theory, and human development.

While there are others to consider, in schools we typically see three approaches used to change adult behavior, which are the authoritarian and transactional approach, the input-and-selection approach, and the democratic approach. Each approach might be used in different situations and in different contexts. Moreover, each approach is influenced by varying degrees of choice, responsibility, and decisionmaking structures for those educators involved (see Table 6.1).

Table 6.1. Choice, Responsibility, and Control

	Authoritarian and Transactional Approach	Input-and-Selection Approach	Democratic Approach
Degree of choice	Low to none	Moderate	High
Degree of responsibility	Low to none	Moderate	High
Decisions made by formal leadership position	High	Moderate	Low to none

In the authoritarian and transactional approach, educators, as well as their grade-level teams or departments, are told what to do, how to do it, and when the work should be accomplished. Often these requirements are connected to maintaining ongoing employment. Formal school leaders using this approach assert their formal authority and control over other professionals in a school building based on what they determine is the best course of action. Typically, behavior is modified with rewards and consequences. Often, authoritarian and transactional leaders mask their leadership by asking for input from advisory roles that give an outward appearance of democratic structures, but final decisions are clearly made by one person for all others and are based on power over subordinates.

In the input-and-selection approach, a leader provides a set of acceptable choices that she/he has predetermined. In some cases, educators may be allowed to suggest alternatives, but ultimately the leader with formal authority decides what is considered an acceptable choice. In this approach, educators have agency in the sense that they can select from a group of predetermined choices, but again, decisions are ultimately made by the leader with formal authority. This is power over others, but allowing limited input and choice.

In the democratic approach, a leader with formal authority is allowed (and expected) to participate in the group decisionmaking process, but hierarchy is flattened and formal authority does not determine decisions. In this approach, all educators, regardless of formal authority, accept the same rights and responsibilities to determine future actions. There is no power over others, but rather an equal distribution of power.

These three approaches provide useful insights into analyzing the existing mental models of educators around change, specifically when looking at decisionmaking structures and how power, choice, and responsibility motivate educators. We know that adult learning theory connects responsibility with choice, and when educators feel choice is absent, they are not motivated to feel responsible for outcomes. As noted in the authoritarian and transactional approach, a leader might have a high level of decisionmaking ability, but she/he takes away choice from other educators. This results in little to no responsibility by the collective body of educators in a building for decisions made on their behalf, and behavior only changes based on incentives or retributions, resulting in a form of professional behaviorism. In the input-and-selection approach, a leader offers some level of choice, but only choices that are considered acceptable to her/him. This bastardizes the idea of input from the faculty, because the decision is ultimately not made by the leader with formal authority and therefore, she/he can disown responsibility and pass blame to the educators who made the "choice." Only the democratic approach requires all educators in a building, regardless of formal authority, to accept responsibility and consequences for making decisions as a collective unit. And it is here that we understand the importance of allowing educators to have choice and responsibility to motivate school renewal and improvement efforts in a community.

So, how does this relate to school renewal? First, in the American public school system, a public school fulfills its highest purpose when democratic decisions are at the heart of teaching and learning. We've made this point in previous chapters, but it is important to reiterate when considering choice, responsibility, and motivation. Voice and input are enormous motivating factors and an important consideration for human resource decisions.

Second, changes to decisionmaking structures are not easy or cut-and-dried situations. They must be negotiated at the building, district, and community level as it would be impossible to make every decision necessary within a school system using the democratic approach. However, deciding when these approaches are used, and in what contexts, is crucial when considering who is ultimately responsible for ensuring that educational change takes place.

Third, and of particular importance for any practitioner reading this book, is to acknowledge that both schools *and* individuals vary in their developmental readiness to embark on the democratic approach and in democratic decisionmaking structures. Not all schools are ready for full democratization, nor are they expected to be. Being able to analyze the developmental needs of a school is crucial to the school renewal process.

DEVELOPMENTAL NEEDS

There are a surprising number of schools in America that have virtually no experience working in cross-departmental or cross-grade-level teams. Often these schools have little to no experience of faculty having the opportunity to give input on schoolwide or districtwide decisions, and outside of social events, there is often little evidence of community input or involvement. In essence, these schools operate as closed systems, where a selective and small group makes decisions on behalf of all students, teachers, and the community at large with no outside input or accountability. Occasionally parts of these closed systems might be made public—discontented teachers leaving or the revolving door of the principal position at a middle school—but the system continues to operate in a closed manner. The system itself might not be aware that it operates in this manner, it has no awareness of any other way to operate, or it doesn't care to change and likes not having to take input and become a more open system.

The type of school just described is the neo-conventional school. In a neo-conventional school, individuals have been conditioned to work in isolation and as a result are not comfortable working in groups. Additionally, educators in this type of school do not like to share ideas or publicly confront policy or practice, usually due to the authoritarian nature of leadership that has valued the pursuit of accountability outcomes. Leadership behaviors in these buildings are typically seen as domineering, stifling discussion, and are sometimes labeled as manipulative or transactional in order to maintain authority. In a neo-conventional school, personal values, beliefs, and concerns around pedagogical practices take a back seat to district-mandated implementation of curriculum to reach or maintain high-stakes testing outcomes.

Neo-conventional schools that have been led by an authoritarian and transactional approach need incremental steps to become more democratic educational systems. Typically, a good first step is to move toward an input-and-selection approach that allows members of the school community to make choices with a bounded set of options. Conversely, schools that have been led predominately with the input-and-selection approach can identify small but important educational issues that can be determined by a democratic approach so that voice and input can begin to be valued. Schools that allow democratic decisions among educators within the building can continue to examine and explore how to increase democratic decisions among students, parents, and community members. There is a continuum to increasing input and voice, but knowing where to start in a school is crucial.

A nuance for school communities to consider is not only the organizational decisionmaking culture, but also individual development levels of thinking about school renewal and change. For example, people with limited thinking—that is, with limited experience and knowledge in a certain area—need more structure from an authority or an expert. This is often true of beginning teachers who need help or assistance for 3 to 5 years before they have mastered aspects of teaching, such as behavior management, differentiated instruction, curriculum development, and so on. More veteran teachers, however, need to be supported in different ways, and so assistance might come in the form of supervision that helps them develop more of a reflective stance about their own instructional practices. The same is true with working toward becoming a more democratic school system. Some people might want someone else to make the decision for them and say, "I don't really care what we do. Just tell me so this meeting can end and I can get out of here." Conversely, there will be some who want to be much

Table 6.2. Developmental Levels of Knowledge and Concern Regarding School Renewal

Experience and Knowledge	Concern and Commitment	Approach toward Democratization
Low	Low	Structured and likely leader led
Mixed	Mixed	Input from various formal and informal leaders
High	High	Completely open sourced

more involved and say, "This is really important to me, and before a decision is made, I'd like to be involved and at the discussion table." Table 6.2 shows the connection among experience, knowledge, concern, and commitment, and the appropriate approach toward becoming a more democratic school system.

By way of review, we offer some quick application of how to interpret Table 6.2. In a school where most members are not very knowledgeable or concerned about school renewal and more broadly the applications of democracy within a school, this will more likely need to start with formal leadership that sees a need and has the formal authority to drive such a shift. In schools that have a mix of knowledge, experience, concern, and commitment toward democratic principles, there will more likely need to be an amalgamation of formal and informal leaders who are interested and willing to develop a school renewal plan that will engage a broader pool of stakeholders. And in schools that already have high levels of experience and concern about democratic principles in school systems, these systems are more likely to be open to leading *with* community groups to address community concerns.

Again, the developmental perspective is really just a lens through which we can view the needs of individuals in order to support schools becoming more democratic institutions. Who currently has the knowledge or commitment to help a school be more democratic? Over time, how do democratic ideals spread throughout a school community? How do we know if commitment is increasing or decreasing, and what does this say about the school renewal process more broadly? These are crucial questions to answer. Just as important, however, is the need to acknowledge sociocultural differences among faculty members and groups, which we address in the next section.

SOCIOCULTURAL DIFFERENCES

How people respond to democratic ideals and principles can largely be attributed to sociocultural differences that are grounded in concepts such as power, control, openness (or lack thereof) to change, and level of inclusiveness.

Concepts of control and power are influenced by various sociocultural factors, which include but are not limited to gender, race, ethnicity, economic status, sexual orientation, age, and national origin, just to name a few. These concepts and factors influence the extent to which people either feel included, excluded, or simply discouraged in participating in a democratic organization. The framework we provide in this book—the promise, the pledge, and the problem-solving process—provides a structure to support community-based school renewal. However, there is much cultural work that needs to be done in each individual school to determine how sociocultural differences will be addressed.

Take gender for example. We know that when girls and boys enter the PK–12 American system, there is no difference in math achievement, and yet by third grade measurable differences on standardized tests of girls scoring lower than boys (Cheema & Galluzzo, 2013) emerge. What causes this change? Is it belief about ability and work ethic? Questions around gender and the roles of educators in schools can and should be raised as well. Why is it that over 75% of our teaching force are women (and White, but we'll get to that in a minute) (Loewus, 2017), while women comprise 54% of all principals (NCES, 2017b) and just 13% of superintendents (Glass, 2000)? Given these gender discrepancies, how can we make sure discussions about gender lead to candid conversations and collaborative decisionmaking? How can we address gender stereotypes to ensure inequities are acknowledged but also to move forward with democratic principles that will strengthen a community? These questions are not about placing blame, but acknowledging inequities and focusing on communication as a vehicle to drive improvement efforts.

Another difference to consider is around race and ethnicity. Race has a powerful influence on how people perceive our collective society in America, particularly as it relates to social structures around power, control, and access. Moreover, ethnicity is interconnected to cultural norms, values, and beliefs. These sociocultural differences are crucial to discuss, openly and honestly, about how a school might function more democratically to better serve a community. Does the school faculty and administration readily question issues of equity around race and ethnicity? Does it model, as a system with power and control, how to question the perceptions of educators to better reflect the diverse group of students and families within a community? With a calm and open conversation, do concepts such as White fragility, the Black Lives Matter movement, and rights to Indigenous peoples' access to land and resources have relevance to what we do? While these are just a few examples of race and ethnicity, the ability to communicate about them openly and honestly, rather than seeing a school system as sociocultural-neutral system, provides authority to educators working on behalf of a community to increase democratic principles.

Other sociocultural differences that influence communication have to do with demographics such as economic status, sexual orientation, age, and national origin. What people experience based on these differences is often deeply rooted in traditions of power and control, which in America have been built for and established by heterosexual White males typically of Anglo-Saxon descent who tend to come from middle-class to upper-class backgrounds. While America is changing and shifting, it is crucial that we attend to and ask questions about power, inclusiveness (or lack thereof), and openness to discuss all of these critical differences. The challenge is determining how to discuss these sensitive but vital matters; the reward is developing group dynamics that can empower a school to become a powerful community force for change.

GETTING STARTED

So, how can educators jump into this work? How can a school start to make a difference in a community? First, we strongly suggest acknowledging the work is likely going to take more time than we might think as people are different and really do vary. Making assumptions (we all know what happens when we assume) about how people perceive the world is dangerous. Rather, we suggest the use of the promise, the pledge, and the problem-solving process as a framework to invite stakeholders to share thoughts and commitment through action. You never really know how powerful the notion of community-based school renewal is until you invite someone to participate.

Second, determine the readiness of a school community when increasing choice, voice, and responsibility. What happens when this occurs? Do people rise to the challenge, or do they avoid it and see it as "extra" work? What are the communication problems that arise, among whom, and because of what sociocultural differences? The ability to acknowledge differences, and work toward a solution to the differences, is a prelude to the work of school renewal itself. In other words, team building and group dynamics occur before and during the school renewal process, and are something that will need to be acknowledged and addressed as the democratic process continues.

Third, take into account the previous history of approaches to leadership that will dictate the developmental needs of a school organization. If a school has experienced mostly authoritarian and transactional approaches to changing adult behavior, democratization and change will likely have to be more structured and slowly introduced. If a school has traditionally operated under the input-and-selection approach, various input from formal and informal leaders can lead to greater shared governance with the developmental goal of a more equal distribution of power. Similarly, if a school has already operated under a democratic approach, then a comprehensive reflection using the promise, the pledge, and the problem-solving process can help further address issues of inequity and increase voice and choice among stakeholders. What needs to be acknowledged in this process is that the work itself is never done, because schools are simply microcosms of society where different groups are constantly asserting power and control over others. It is the work of the school to address these issues and disrupt comfort.

THE NEED TO IDENTIFY AND ACT ON INEQUITY

Schools have a moral imperative to use the collective intelligence within the school organization to address inequities. Through new roles, relationships, and reflections, we can better work together to self-renew our commitment to each other and to *all* stakeholders in the community. Anything less than that is undemocratic.

Make no mistake about it, shared governance takes time and effort. It also produces some heartache and frustration. However, when we learn to work together, we give the gift of voice, not only to each other as educators but also to our students, our parents, and the community more broadly. With this gift comes empowerment—not power over a community but power to those who have historically had their voices silenced or ignored. It is the collective voice, the voice that says what we all need in order to be successful, that binds us together and makes us stronger.

In order for this reality to come to fruition, educators and community members alike are going to need to examine their mental models about what a school "is" and dream about what a school "could be." Like Plato's parable of the cave, there are many shadows that will be scary for us to address. What fears do we have that prevent us from being a stronger community? What are the sources of our fears and the assumptions we make as a result of these fears? How can we help each other see the difference between the shadows that are cast against our walls and the reality we can create together? These questions cannot be answered by principals and superintendents, nor can they be answered by school board members, parents, students, and teachers. To become more democratic, we must first disrupt what our systems have been told to do by dictated policy and practice over the past several decades. In most cases, this will be uncomfortable, but it will also identify inequities that can be addressed in action. Collectively, community-based decisions can help school systems learn, implement, adjust, and continue the self-improvement cycle. And once a school organization has begun the process, the shadows cast will become less fearful the more enlightened a community becomes.

CHAPTER 7

Dealing with Tough Questions of Practice

With the promise, pledge, and problem-solving process framework, we hope educators will be better equipped to take into account the developmental and sociocultural needs of the community their school system serves. It is with this three-dimensional framework that educators can begin the real work of democratizing schools, namely breaking away from instruction directly aligned to external assessment and prepackaged curriculum, and increasing coaching that is focused on developing reflective stances around teaching practices. Changing routine is not easy, but if we want to deal with tough questions about practices in our schools, we will need to navigate uncharted waters together in rethinking positions, roles, and responsibilities in our school systems.

Organizational analysis, whether in business, health care, or education, shows that it is better to walk toward conflict than to move away from it. Conflict highlights important issues that need to be discussed and the very real consequences change can bring about. With democratizing our school systems, civil public conflict about how schools best serve a community should be seen as a good sign. This allows for strong differences of opinion to be aired in the open rather than hearing only from the most dominant voices in a school system or in the community. When there is open conflict, schools and communities are able to bring light to hidden conflicts, reducing the likelihood of subversion if voices about what constitutes good instruction and learning are suppressed. The goal, then, is to find productive conflict that leads to a debate of opinions and open discussions about what is needed to better serve the community. Once these debates have occurred, and agreements have been reached, a community and the school system it serves are better able to work together to maximize function and minimize unexpected and destructive conflict.

Embedded at the core of school renewal is the focus on how to turn *ideological* conflict into productive change—not for individuals to attack each other with insults and turn disagreement into *personal* conflict. The democratization of American PK–12 schools is to acknowledge differing opinions, allow for disagreement of ideas, and find constructive ways to turn ideological conflict into agreed-upon middle ground. While tension is not always comfortable, it is to be expected and focused on as a source of progress—through conflict, schools and communities can learn to walk in unison to strengthen bonds with each other rather than focusing on conflicting priorities.

School renewal does not have an easy or clear-cut path. In fact, it is often filled with potholes and roots that are easy to trip over (see Fahey, Breidenstein, Ippolito, & Hensley, 2019). However, there are ways to avoid some of these pitfalls, which we describe in the following pages.

WITH FREEDOM COMES RESPONSIBILITY

For the better part of the last decade as accountability measures have ramped up, educators have been complaining rightfully about their lack of autonomy in providing the educational supports needed to best serve their community and their students. As a result, conflicts and tensions have built up between teachers and student, teachers and administrators, and schools and their communities.

If we want freedom from external authorities, and if we want autonomy to determine best educational practices, then we must accept the responsibility for documenting our effectiveness in a different way. In order to advocate for more inclusive curriculum, documenting student success outside traditional realms of assessment, and thinking differently about the use of resources to better meet the needs of students, we must accept that no external authority can tell us what we can or cannot do. If the community is involved, engaged, and sees value in how a school system contributes to the health of a community, then we have the responsibility *and* the freedom to better our schools. In developing a more collective will to change, we need to also ask deeper questions about our own traditional educational practices.

Messages About the Value of Classes

Increasingly, school systems are funneling students into classes that offer more instructional time for reading and math, mostly in response to poor test scores. While this response provides additional exposure to tested material, it also takes away time from elective classes that are often of high interest to students. A secondary effect of this intervention is that students who come from low-socioeconomic status (SES) backgrounds are often disproportionately pulled out of elective classes, resulting in a form of de facto tracking.

Over time, these practices send messages about classes that are considered "more valuable" than other classes and can create conflicts between educators who teach different subjects. These practices also send the message to students that because they don't perform well on a test, their input into their own learning matters less than that of others. Schools that want to become more democratic will need to ask important questions about the messages the school system sends about the perceived value of classes. How much input does a student have on choosing his or her own areas of interest in learning? What are the messages being sent to both teachers and students about the perceived value of one class over another? How can schools think differently about ensuring supports are given to each individual student while still allowing their voices to be heard and reflected in the electives they choose? How can schools minimize ability grouping but still provide for individual and group attention according to student needs?

Community-Curricula Connections

Almost every PK–12 American school is structured by separate subjects with separate learning times, which inherently creates learning silos and creates disconnects for students. The lack of connection between subjects becomes magnified when topics learned in school do not translate into life outside of school in the community. Not only does this lead to isolated learning, but it does not allow the school system to highlight and honor the value it can bring to the development of a local community.

In order to make connections about what is being learned in school to the community more broadly, schools need to ask important pedagogical and andragogical questions (Drago-Severson, 2009). Does what is being learned in school reflect important knowledge for citizens within the community? Do the pedagogical practices of a school translate into adult development considerations of how adults learn in the outside world? In what ways do interdisciplinary questions addressed in school impact questions or topics being asked within the community? Does the compartmentalized model of learning in finite blocks of time translate into the best ways for students to learn and how they will solve problems once they leave the school?

Project-Based Learning

Since the early 19th century, American public schools have used grades as a way to rank and sort students. Additionally, grades often have a more nefarious outcome in the attempt to standardize and normally distribute achievement, which often negatively influences immigrant children and students from low-SES and minority backgrounds. While grades have become widely internalized in PK–12 American education (even proficiency-based rankings often result in de facto grades), school systems could do more to think about the importance of applying knowledge in context to project-based learning (PBL) experiences.

School systems, particularly those trying to become more democratic, could provide more PBL opportunities. Students from a wide variety of grades could come together and be given a task where they have to solve a problem using teamwork and various pieces of background knowledge. In this PBL structure, how can work be assessed to reflect what students know and apply in practice? How could this assessment value performance and application, not simply time spent sitting in a seat? How might schools think differently about using PBL structures to address problems occurring in a community that result in a performance and display back to the community? How might these PBL structures inform future community decisions?

Multimedia Resources and Use of Technology

Traditionally, schools have spent an inordinate amount of instructional money on computerized instruction, traditional textbooks, and consumable workbooks, many of which are published by the same companies that also write standardized tests. What has resulted is an overreliance on textbooks and digitized resources provided by textbook companies. How many adults go to an academic text to find answers to an everyday question? In this day of the Internet, not many. Democratic schools know that learning in the real world almost always occurs outside of four walls.

The renewal of American schools should encourage students to find information from a variety of resources in order to determine their own understanding of a topic or idea. Schools need to teach students how to gather information responsibly, not attempt to control the predetermined outcomes for students. How does a school encourage exploration of topics? How does the use of multimedia resources encourage students to remain naturally inquisitive and ask questions about topics? How does this type of learning contribute to an informed society that is interested in healthy dialogue about differences of opinions? How should a school disseminate information learned through the use of various electronic platforms?

Creative Use of Staffing

A well-established budgeting reality is that roughly 80% of an operating budget is spent on funding for personnel. While staff assignments are important for helping a school run smoothly (think of what might happen without secretaries or custodians), role specialization can and should be reconceptualized as we move further into the 21st century. Teachers will almost always be needed to teach specific subjects, counselors will need to help address socioemotional needs of students, and administrators will need to help with leadership initiatives and managerial considerations.

That being said, schools also need to think about creative use of staffing by streamlining existing use of full-time employees (FTE) to free up funding in the budget to address what is needed by the organization more broadly. How might a home-school communicator be used to engage with segments of the community that have historically felt disenfranchised by a school district? Would hiring a social worker help address trauma experienced by a growing population of the community? How would an instructional coach be used to help teachers develop more of a reflective stance about instructional practices?

Rethinking the Schedule

Although schools have struggled with scheduling issues for decades, there remains a need to continue to think about—and seek out the research on—how the daily school schedule impacts student learning. How much recess time is needed for younger students to maintain high levels of learning? When should high school students start their day based on brain research? How can structured breaks, including mindfulness activities, actually lead to more intense and focused learning sessions? In schools that use teams, should there be bell systems or should there be more flexibility to meet targeted instructional needs?

The use of time, and the development of a schedule, has been deeply embedded in the factory model of a school learning system. However, schools don't make quarterly earnings, so why should they be based on quarters or even semesters? Additionally, summer vacation is based on the tradition of an agrarian model, but less than 1% of students take part in the agriculture industry in America, so why do we still have extended summer vacations? Should schools have weekly professional development half-days to support teacher learning, and if so, what supports can the community offer students who wouldn't be in school at that time? Is there a need to expand the school day past the existing schedule, and if so, how might this be negotiated with the teachers' union through the collective bargaining process?

MORAL AUTHORITY; NOT IMPOSED FORMAL AUTHORITY

By this point in the accountability experiment, we should have a pretty good understanding about schoolwide change and community improvement, namely that change must come from within if we are to improve outcomes for students. While formal authority, often imposed by outside agencies, can force changes to practices and policies through economic levers, it is the moral authority of educators and the community more broadly that will answer tough questions about how to better prepare citizens and contribute to community development. If we want a better democracy, one with civility and an educated and engaged citizen base, we need to model a framework of democratic principles that values problem solving, community-based promises, and pledges that we make to one another. How might changes provide educational benefits? What debates should we openly have to determine governance and decisionmaking around inputs and outputs of community-based schools? Why is it important to value all voices in the democratic process, even if the stance or opinion is one that the collective group does not adopt? Even when there is great disagreement in the governance process of a school, it is a far better way to serve a community than having no input and being forced to implement outside mandates. By giving people in a community the chance to express their opinion, enthusiasm about what *might be* begins to replace *what currently is*.

To be clear, we want to make sure we are not advocating for individualism and siloed classroom instruction. Schoolwide change does not occur simply because people are given more autonomy or are allowed to function in small faculty groups. To truly impact a community and increase democratic ideals, school renewal comes when an entire school is able to work toward a common purpose in congruence with moral authority and collective leadership. When school change is attempted through pilot programs without an endorsement of the school governance system, unresolved tension remains where faculty groups can vie for power through individual interests rather than for a common good. Even if there's no tension between faculty, there's an equity tension if the programs are only for a select group of students or if only a few teachers commit to implementing the program. In order to produce school renewal, educators need to be able to study each other's work, visit and observe instruction, participate in group development tasks, and have a voice in updating practices and protocols. Rather than implementing new initiatives, we must take the initiative to study ourselves and create an understanding of who we are as a school system to better support our community.

DIVERSIFICATION VS. COMPETITION

While schools need to have a collective common purpose to help drive community development and improvement, that does not mean that every school should be the same or have the same promise or pledge. In fact, school renewal should be based on the notion that democratization is based on the individualized needs of the community the school serves. That said, there continues to be a belief that schools, like businesses, will be made better through competition. For schools, this includes comparing achievement scores and athletic prowess, which can become quite sensitive information as these are published in newspapers and through various social media. In many states, schools are ranked not only by state departments of education, but also in people's minds, and they impact real-estate property and funding formulas.

However, what if schools focused less on competition and more on diversification with each other? By diversifying policies and practices that align more to the needs of individual communities rather than with state or federal mandates, schools would be able to tackle significant local issues facing students and parents more broadly, leading to better support structures and learning outcomes. And diversification doesn't mean that schools don't observe each other—quite the opposite, in fact, leading to increased observations about what other school systems are doing so they can learn from each other about diversity in action. In doing so, schools can take what others are doing and adapt it to better meet their own community needs, and not have fear about comparison or reprisals when they don't meet a one-size-fits-all imposed mandate.

In order to move beyond the climate of competition, schools that choose to move ahead with school renewal need to be prepared to deal with criticism and incorporate community ideas in order to develop a unique vision of learning and teaching. Whenever a school advocates for itself, initially, it is likely to be attacked by other schools and ostracized rather than praised and supported; and this is for a variety of reasons that have to deal with power, control, finances, and embedded comfort levels of those who work for a school system. School systems (typically central office personnel and school board officials) resent hearing about unusual or progressive education because it can lead to internal attempts at change. Principals (particularly those with a managerial paradigm) don't like to hear about other leaders who value empowering others in shared decisionmaking because it challenges notions of power and control. Teachers (usually those who work in hierarchical districts) do not like to hear that other teachers have the ability to alter curriculum, use different assessments, and use more time-intensive instructional methods to engage students because it highlights that change can happen for educators who are willing to confront practices within a school system. However, if a school is truly meant to support *and* serve a community, change is necessary.

For those schools that do move ahead with school renewal, educators will also need to listen to unsettling questions from outside as well as from within. These questions will include "Why should we change anything in our school?," "If we change the way we instruct, won't some of our kids suffer academically?," or even "Who does this change best serve?" All of these questions are important to answer; however, of equal importance is the question of how a school that is struggling with the core purpose of education should study other schools in order to diversify practices and policies to best meet community needs. Below are suggestions for schools to consider as democratic principles are investigated:

1. Listen carefully to the criticism that is being offered and decide on its merit. Is the critique a result of someone's effort and hard

work being challenged? Should certain efforts be recognized and publicized more openly as a positive reason that more effort should be made to achieve change? Which traditions should be honored and valued that don't require change and would lead to worse outcomes for students if abandoned, and who determines these traditions?
2. Build reflective leadership communities that focus on the mobilization of educators and community members, specifically the successes and struggles of empowering democratic principles. In what ways have people been inspired to accept change? How have others derailed change? Who have the leaders been, both formal and informal, that have helped promote change? What protocols of a shared decisionmaking process have been used successfully, and which ones need to be revisited?
3. Acknowledge collaborative efforts with other school systems to establish observation protocols that will lead to trusting reflections rather that competitive criticism. No school is without its warts and blemishes, so how can schools learn from each other in honest ways and thus help empathize with difficult realities? How can practices be observed in a manner that allows for diversification rather than negative comparisons? How can educators have honest conversations with educators outside the school system that foster deep reflections with coworkers?

In short, to support each other in becoming more democratic institutions, schools should be able to learn from each other how they can diversify to better meet community needs, not be more competitive with each other. In demystifying this process, educators should be open about the challenges of addressing criticism and reducing defensiveness. In doing so, schools can re-democratize themselves by realizing they are all in the same boat as they attempt to determine what works best for their students, their parents, and their communities.

THE ABILITY OF A PRINCIPAL TO MOBILIZE

When attempting to lead a school going through the renewal process, a principal will be judged not on her or his ability to manage others, but on her or his ability to mobilize and inspire others in action. It is a position that requires a deep understanding of psychology, the ability to motivate and coach others, and the desire to transform traditional American perspectives about leadership in our PK–12 public schools. However, many educational leaders have been ill-prepared by preparation programs to consider interpersonal and intrapersonal challenges of leadership, and many do not have mentorship support once they are in a leadership position to act as anything other than a manager who is simply implementing district policy. For most average Americans, it is hard to accept that a principal can and even should be democratic. Usually the most visible public figure in any PK–12 American public school, the principal is often a lightning rod for controversy and disparaging remarks.

That said, many successful leaders (principals and teachers alike) realize that if they are to harness moral authority, and if they are to better meet the needs of *all* the children who attend their school, then they must be able to inspire others to think differently and change practices. As a result, successful democratic principals are able to mobilize others with statements such as these:

- "I, as a principal, chose to engage in a democratic process where I value power with rather than power over."
- "I, as a principal, am legally and ultimately responsible for decisions in our school; however, I have a developed a system that determines the level of teacher input and only use my formal authority when completely necessary."
- "I, as a principal, share a collective responsibility to see that the best educational decisions possible are made and in the spirit of what is best for students and for the community, not for adults working in the school."
- "I, as a principal, am willing to lose a decision because my voice is not more important than others, and I realize that I cannot lead alone if I want to create trust among our faculty."
- "I, as a principal, may struggle to lead in a democratic fashion and with the concept that it is easier to just tell teachers what to do; however, I realize our democratic principles start with me."

Obviously, a single person is not responsible for all the accolades or criticism for attempting to renew a school to be more democratic. So it is important for school renewal to be represented by a variety of people besides the principal, people who have been empowered to mobilize others to represent a schoolwide and community effort.

OPPORTUNITIES TO ENGAGE THE LARGER COMMUNITY

Schools face an age-old problem regarding perceptions of how they function because most Americans attended an American PK–12 system. In fact, public school systems are one of the few socialized institutions that most Americans can say they have experienced for a large majority of their formative years. When it comes to change, however, the American public can be highly critical, either because they don't want change, they feel they know what is needed for change, or they feel school was a negative experience that was done *to* them and they don't want the same thing to happen to their child or children. Whatever the reasoning, when a school starts to have discussions about changes, educators should expect to have negative reactions from the community.

If students are to be engaged with real and impactful work that will contribute to community development, community members will have to be part of the discussion about how this might look and translate into practice. Community-based learning, flexible use of time, and new forms of demonstrating knowledge (note we do not use the term "test" or "assessment," per se) all require collaboration and discussion to occur with parents, community groups, and stakeholders to bridge the gap between learning in the four walls of the school and application in the societal ecosystem of the community. And it is here that the work becomes interesting and an *opportunity*, and does not need to be labeled as a challenge. While the general public has been led to believe that schools are disconnected and instruments of domination, in reality many educators simply want to help develop children but feel constricted by external mandates. Instead of being pitted against each other, schools and communities can walk toward each other and begin to have conversations about values, beliefs, and expectations for how they might better work together to support the same outcome: children who are productive, engaged, and caring. Innovation doesn't come from above; it comes from the minds and hard work of educators and people within the community.

We don't want to sugarcoat the process of renewing schools in America—it won't be easy and many members of the community will likely resist the effort at first. However, with time, conversations, and a true effort to work together, schools can envision and imagine the important role they play in human development, learning outcomes, and the contribution to society more broadly. The challenge can be met with opportunity and optimism—and the equity-oriented focus of how schools can help develop communities to rise to the challenges of the 21st century.

WHY OPPORTUNITIES ARE AT THE HEART OF RENEWING AMERICAN SCHOOLS

A school, with its pledge, makes a commitment to parents, students, and community members to make decisions that will help support and develop a community. Additionally, a school makes a promise around principles of learning and teaching to help optimize the educational environment. And, through the problem-solving process, schools engaged in school renewal use community-based action research to drive student learning that is directly

Dealing with Tough Questions of Practice

applicable to community outcomes. When these work in harmony, the work of students and teachers flows in and out of the school and into the community effortlessly. However, there are often critical moments that have to first occur to reach this point, and in the moment, educators might feel as though they are taking a step back in the process. That said, these points in time provide the foundation for renewal to occur. Below are some critical moments we have observed in school renewal that are important for educators to consider through their own process.

Critical Moment #1: Losing to Gain

Perhaps the most critical moment of the school renewal process is when the community (either within the school or the community more broadly) realizes that the governing process truly is democratic and not autocratic. Often this occurs when the principal, the formal leader of the school building, fails to win support for a decision she or he has strongly backed. Typically, these moments are not seen in schools, but in a school that values democratic ideals, values, and beliefs, this type of event allows others, intellectually, emotionally, and spiritually, to understand the school renewal process is for real. Often this occurs when the principal has made her or his opposition known, and has openly fought hard to convince and influence others, but publicly states and acknowledges, "I disagree with the decision. I don't think this is the way we can best serve our community, but as a member of this group, one who has the same decisionmaking authority for this issue, I will support the choice of the group and work as hard as I can to make it successful."

Critical Moment #2: Addressing Group Dynamics

The governance structure is being completely ignored in a meeting, and people are arguing and even assessing blame as to why the issue exists in the first place. Rather than hearing each other's point of view, individuals seem more interested in winning a debate point. The meeting ends when some members of the faculty get up and walk out of the room. The critical moment comes at the next meeting, when one of the group members clearly and calmly addresses what happened last time by saying, "Last meeting was not good for any of us. Rather than trying to figure out how we can work together, we got tangled up in an argument. I've been thinking a lot, and I reached out to some of you in this room afterward to apologize for the role I know I played last time. If we can't work together, how can we expect our community to be able to work with us? I know we all don't see eye to eye, but we do have to figure out how to work together and get on the same sheet of music. Can we commit as a faculty to engage, speak up, and listen to each other? Can we all work toward this goal together?" Rather than ignoring past issues, productive groups address their frustrations with each other and make commitments to work together so that better group dynamics emerge.

Critical Moment #3: Organizational Vulnerability

In spite of the efforts to be more inclusive and bring in community members to help address issues in the community, a school going through the renewal process is fending off private and public attacks from members in the community. Traditionally, schools have circled the wagons and used policies and procedures to weaponize their responses. Often, this results in the school organization engaging in a process of "we're right, you're wrong," and pushes members of the school community further away from each other rather than addressing the source of the conflict. Instead, schools need to practice organizational vulnerability, where they (educators) actively engage in listening, understanding, and discussion with the members of the public who are engaging in the attacks, often through newspapers and on social media. With a calm response that acknowledges the opposing opinion, school officials can be open to suggestions and ask for input on how to address a situation without compromising morals or beliefs. While there will always be speed bumps in the democratization of a school system, educational organizations can learn a lot from the public by listening and acknowledging rather than engaging in arguments.

Critical Moment #4: Bridging the Gap Between Ideal and Reality

It is one thing to think about re-democratizing a school, and even to develop formalized plans for implementation, but it is a completely different level of work to consistently address and adapt what is ideal and what can be done in reality. Seemingly, when consensus on the ideal is reached, the immediate implementation of a plan might break down due to miscommunication or lack of follow-up. Some might think, "It would just be easier if we stuck with what we have always done." However, we know that what is easiest for educators isn't always what is best for students, and we certainly know that what we are doing now in our schools isn't what is best for our democracy. As with every shift or change, the critical shift in the process comes when individual fears are replaced with collective support within the group. Once this happens, a group has begun to form a bond that, with some nurturing, is the foundation to bridging the gap between theory and reality.

THE CONTINUUM OF RENEWAL

School renewal is not a linear process (Fahey et al., 2019). It is something that ebbs and flows, has surges and lulls, and can be apparent one moment and invisible the next. And what is likely to be the most challenging for Americans is that it is inherently a communal process rather than one that values the individual. That being said, school renewal requires us to tap into the energy of human emotions, beliefs, rhythms, values, and work ethic to devote ourselves to ensuring the children of the community we serve have a powerful educational experience. And that can only occur when democratic learning principles are present.

CHAPTER 8

Supporting School Renewal
Important Signals from the District

Democracies and moral enterprises (such as education systems tasked with helping develop responsible and educated citizens) do not function well under autocratic leadership. In fact, democracies wither and die under uniform mandates that don't directly serve local constituents.

In order to accomplish this major paradigm shift, support from leadership at the district level will be needed to help signal an institutional change. Without support from the central office there can be no long-term rethinking and restructuring of how schools function at the local or neighborhood level. Important questions and issues about power, control, and responsibility will have to be addressed, including how a school district shifts from a lens of centralized control to one of democratic community that works together, much like the different branches of government. In doing so, district-level leaders can help provide structure and support to create collective autonomy.

In re-democratizing our schools, policies and practices will need to strike a balance between autonomy and structure, where various factions, including school boards, teachers' unions, administrators, and teachers, learn how to better work together rather than compete with one another to best support local stakeholders.

Schools best serve their students and their parents when they are collaborative, open their doors to the public, and engage with their stakeholders to determine values, beliefs, and targeted outcomes for students. This is at the heart of America's history, where educators attempt to provide quality public education that will create an informed citizenry. It takes time and collaboration, not mandates and requirements pushed down people's throats. And it requires all members of the school system to understand the shift we need to make if we are to ensure our future is able to access and implement democratic principles.

THE POLITICS OF A SCHOOL BOARD AND DISTRICT PERSONNEL

Increasingly since the advent of the accountability movement, school boards and district-level leaders have played larger roles in the process of impacting what happens at the school level with daily instructional practices. This has happened as centralized accountability practices have transitioned to centralized efforts to control instruction in order to produce outcomes on standardized tests. And it should be mentioned there are now major changes going on in broadening assessments beyond single test scores that states and districts should be aware of (Fair Test, 2019).

Traditionally, a school board's role has been to set policies and negotiate the political process to ensure that schools have enough resources to provide quality instructional experiences to students. The district's role has been to coordinate and implement assistance to schools from the balcony perspective, particularly to ensure equitable instructional experiences occur across a district population. As we move further into the 21st century, and our economy moves further away from the 19th-century mentality of industrial production, our schools will need to adjust how support is provided to foster creativity, innovation, and response in real time.

To be clear, we don't want to sound naïve, but we think both school boards and district-level personnel need to give up significant control in order to help produce better localized outcomes for students and their parents. The job of both the school board and district-level leaders should operate more as a commission, where the role is to help define and solidify core beliefs and values about teaching and learning, define goals and outcomes for what it means to be educated within the system, provide money and resources to allow for localized control around teaching and learning, and help teachers and administrators with each school reflect on how and whether progress is being made. They should only intervene in the instructional operations of a school if they are asked to do so by the school itself, when a school is not prepared or able to make a decision by itself, or when mutually agreed-upon progress is not being made.

School boards and district personnel can play vital roles in our American democracy. They provide critical support for assisting schools with the internal work of determining quality teaching and learning. They can play the role of advocate in the community when people outside of the school renewal process are doubtful or critical. They can declare their trust in the school community's process, which can add to the credibility of the process.

OPPORTUNITIES TO EMPOWER

There could be so much gained if a district were to empower schools to meet the individualized needs of students rather than respond to standardized pressures. To accomplish this work, however, schools would have to be willing and able to operate and accept certain givens, which would allow school boards and district-level leaders to provide more leeway and autonomy to function within responsible and legal parameters. These givens include:

- Abiding by constitutional law
- Addressing issues of inequity
- Sensitivity for differentiated needs
- Valuing practical research
- Progressing toward agreed-upon district goals
- Including local accountability measures
- Continuing updates to the promise, pledge, and problem solving through action research

Again, these givens could be used to work within established district priorities and made public through the governance process. *Constitutional law* simply means that whatever a school decides to do does not violate a state or federal law, such as not discriminating against a student based on race, ethnicity, gender, and so on. *Addressing issues of inequity* means that educational decisions are made to ensure inequities are addressed and that a school system does not favor one group of students at the expense of another and that achievement gaps between groups are addressed and narrowed. *Sensitivity for differentiated needs* implies that all students, regardless of demographics, have needs that must be incorporated into teaching and learning to help them connect with curricula, which could include identities around race, ethnicity, culture, sexual orientation, and learning disabilities. *Valuing practical research* is defined as the use of practitioner-friendly research to support policies and decisions as they relate to instruction, learning, behavior support structures, and social–emotional needs. *Progress toward agreed-upon district goals* implies that a school's decisions will address the priorities of local stakeholders and be made collectively by parents, students, and educators. *Local accountability measures* refers to the previously mentioned district goals to be made public and to engage the public through meetings, printed technical reports, and local publications about the progress being made toward identified objectives and priorities. Lastly, *continual updates to the promise, pledge, and problem solving through action research* refers to the democratic governance process, focus on teaching and learning, and systematic review and self-study of practices. Here is the beauty to these givens: If individual schools accept them and use them to develop plans to meet these givens, then the details and the programs that are implemented are really up to the individualized schools. These give opportunities to schools to gain more control over what they do within the school day and still meet the needs of students.

Imagine, for a second, how these givens might positively impact the culture of a school building. Schools could use different teaching materials, organize remediation and enrichment differently, and staff differently from other schools in the same district *to meet the needs of their students*. Assessments could be more focused *for* student learning rather than *of* student learning (Stiggins, Arter, Chappuis, & Chappuis, 2004), and curriculum could vary from school to school without the use of pacing guides so long as teachers were held accountable to the locally agreed-upon givens. Schools could be free to enter into their own agreements with agencies through memorandums of understanding (MOUs) to address grant-funded opportunities, increase access to community services, and collaborate with businesses to produce community-based outcomes. The district's role in this kind of unshackling would be to empower schools (rather than control them) to provide information and link potential services, analyze common needs, and coordinate activities that can provide evidence of success and develop future implementation plans.

Does this sound exciting or like anarchy to you? It might be based on where your school is in being prepared to engage in this type of community-oriented work. However, wherever your school is in the process, there are infinite numbers of opportunities to gain from the school renewal process and from district-level leaders and school boards helping support schools become more democratic and community focused. This kind of work has purpose, and in order to accomplish the goal of increasing democracy, there must be signals from both the school board and the central office that the work is valued, supported, and structured in a manner that supports collective autonomy.

AN AGE-OLD ISSUE: EQUALITY VS. EQUITY

Before we delve any further into the policies and practices from the district perspective that might help with school renewal, we should address the (mis)conception that all schools must have equal treatment to ensure all students are taught exactly alike. Many school systems (or maybe more accurately their superintendents) make the false assumption that equal treatment will result in equal justice. However, these leaders often lack a more nuanced view of issues of inequity, instead expressing equality as "We do not discriminate in our school district. We teach all students, regardless of where they come from in our town/city, the same. We ensure that all students receive the same treatment, the same programs, the same curriculum, the same textbooks, and the same use of time. Fifth-grade instruction in one building is the same across the whole district." The idea, while well intentioned, is dated and once again takes on a 19th-century perspective about instruction. We know more now about what it means to be equitable rather than ensuring equality, and if we want a healthy democracy where we can provide remediation and enrichment to our students, we need to address this perspective about how schools function.

To be fair to students (to be equitable), we need to stop assuming everyone needs the same thing for instruction (to provide equality). In other words, we need to be more concerned about the *fairness of outcomes* instead of the *sameness of treatment*. Controlling for uniformity in schools hurts students and teaches toward the middle. What community wants "middle of the road" results for their children? In order to meet the needs of all students, we must meet them where they are, challenge them with motivating instruction that they can directly apply to their lives outside of school, and provide opportunities for all students to become productive and democratic citizens. In this regard, the role of a school board and district leadership is to address the concern for fairness by allowing willing schools to have the latitude to produce equitable results, keeping structure and consistent programs in place for schools currently unable or unwilling to initiate, and adjusting resources to account for equity of results.

When a school district makes an adjustment of resources to serve its most impoverished schools and students, it is publicly acknowledging that unequal treatment is in fact the fairest action. Districts that allocate the same amount of funds or resources without acknowledging preexisting economic conditions are merely perpetuating inequities in communities through the education system. It is a moral and democratic decision to support high-poverty schools to become attractive places of learning that support different needs and backgrounds. By offering additional resources, nicer facilities, and incentives to faculty and staff, PK–12 American school systems can play a crucial role in community development. While perhaps politically challenging or unpopular, school districts can honor the challenges that low-income schools face by openly discussing issues of inequity, how these relate to community support and engagement, and simultaneously acknowledge that the challenges of high-income schools are different than those faced by low-income schools. Not every school within the district needs to be implementing the exact same programs/approaches/initiatives. This way no one is neglected, but different challenges are addressed in a manner that is democratic based on student populations.

DEMOCRATIC USE OF ECONOMIC PRINCIPLES

Resource allocation at the district level is important, but what can district-level leaders do to encourage creative and innovative improvements that will lead to school renewal? One concept that is increasingly being applied through public–private partnerships is the use of seed money to fund collaborative improvement efforts. The idea is that seed money, which could come from a small percentage of the school budget or be funded through local business sponsorships, be used to support improvement efforts that could be used to plan, implement, or analyze school change initiatives.

Seed money doesn't need to start off as a large amount. A certain percentage of discretionary funds provided to the school can be useful in helping start an improvement initiative. However, with each year and with outcomes tied to benchmarks seen as valuable by the school district or collaborative community partner, additional funds could be targeted to grow a program. Over time, and in alignment with community development goals, programs targeting schools with high levels of poverty can become something that is given ongoing budget support based on support from parents and other community groups.

If a district is not able to support small amounts of seed money, and there are no local businesses willing to sponsor the funds, grant funding is another option to pursue. There are many small grant opportunities that districts may apply for, and whether it is seed money or a small grant, these additional resources are largely symbolic in that they support the notion of change. In what ways might a school acknowledge the extra time and work that are involved with making a school more democratic? How might schools reengage with a community to show support for the development of students? Attempting to answer these questions encourages educators and community members alike to focus on developing a plan to support school renewal.

DEVELOPING A DISTRICT PLAN FOR SCHOOL RENEWAL

A district plan for school renewal is multifaceted and dynamic. The plan should openly acknowledge that there are different levels of school readiness based on needs of students, experiences of teachers, and leadership abilities of principals. It should also openly communicate with schools about readiness for autonomy and with input from principals and teachers. Those that are ready and willing should be provided with special linking services and structures. For those schools that are not ready, existing district regulation needs to be continued and support needs to be provided. As schools go through the renewal process, learning from each other is a crucial component of organizational improvement. Lastly, protecting the autonomy of each school as a special and unique educational entity helps keep schools as bedrocks of our democracy and improves teaching and learning.

Acknowledge Different Levels of Readiness

Before the school renewal process even begins, district-level leaders need to acknowledge the different needs of students, experiences of teachers, and leadership abilities of principals. History, traditions, norms, and routines are embedded in every school, and school renewal cannot be forced on any faculty, but must be determined internally if a school of educators is ready and willing to move forward with self-governance around schoolwide changes. Some schools are immediately ready to take part in the renewal process, while others simply won't see the need to change. For the latter, the school district needs to provide ongoing support, time, and exposure to the idea of increased autonomy at the school level to better meet the needs of students, their parents, and community expectations more broadly.

Openly Communicate About Readiness

Assumptions about readiness for school renewal will likely lead to misfires in the democratization process. The best way to determine if a school is ready to engage in the change process is to openly communicate with teachers and principals about their perceived readiness. The following are good questions to consider:

- What criteria for self-governance have been in place in the school up to this point?
- Are the district givens acceptable parameters for the school to work within?
- What areas would the district need to decentralize for the school to make better decisions about funding, evaluation, curriculum, and so on?
- What specific resources and assistance will the school need from the district to achieve autonomy?
- How will the school work with the community it serves to hold itself accountable for student results?
- What structures will be used by the principal(s) and the faculty to engage with parents and students in the community?

While full commitment from the principal is critical to school renewal success, just as important is the commitment of faculty and staff. A secret ballot vote among teachers is an important safety valve to help prevent undue influence or pressure from an administrator. Either way, no school should proceed with schoolwide autonomy unless both the principal and staff are for it.

Provide Linking Services and Structures

As mentioned earlier, seed money is a form of resource that can aid in the planning and implementation of school renewal. However, important human resources and structures can and should be provided from the district to help coordinate increased autonomy activities. Teams of educators (teachers and administrators) and community members (students, parents, and stakeholders) should be brought together by a district contact to support and facilitate discussions around changes to policies and practices within the school. The district leader can help synthesize needs assessments, gather information from focus groups, and monitor discussions based on other school renewal processes that occur throughout the district. By formally linking the schools across the district, central office personnel can gather and disseminate information across the community as well as help coordinate on-site professional development at the request of each school.

Continue Existing District Regulations and Supports

Wholesale and rapid change is almost never a good idea, and if the district wants to support and establish ongoing change to policies and practices, it has to continue providing traditional support structures until a school indicates it is ready for complete autonomy. Until a school gives that signal, school districts are still responsible for teacher evaluation programs, curriculum development, reporting procedures, staff development, hiring practices, and other established district standards. For those schools not ready for renewal, all formal district standards and regulations should stay in effect, not as a punitive measure, but to ensure organizational transition is smooth and uninterrupted.

Learning as Organizational Improvement

In order to support organizational improvement, schools need to be able to learn from each other as they engage in the renewal process. This means that the school district has the responsibility to bring schools together and share firsthand knowledge and experiences about attempting to become self-governing. Even schools that have opted not to participate can and should take part in the learning process of what it takes to increase democratic principles in a school building.

District-level leaders can help facilitate the learning process by coordinating visits with other school districts, collecting information and research on other schools going through the renewal process, and actively influencing public perception through news outlets and on social media. By helping identify new, exciting, and valuable practices in schools, district leaders can remediate some of the challenges of the school renewal process. In this manner, district leadership serves as a facilitator of democratic principles and of learning more broadly, modeling the type of leadership that principals can emulate at the building level.

Protecting Autonomy as a Bedrock of Democracy

Perhaps the most important function a district can provide is the protection of autonomy to its schools. If a district is concerned with supporting schools in the development of productive citizens in a democracy, then its focus should be on creating the parameters for this development and then allowing each building to meet the individual needs of the community it serves. By allowing schools to exercise their own moral and professional judgments, the district is supporting, encouraging, and assisting the schools rather than suppressing them by a centralized bureaucracy. And this is at the heart of American principles.

FADE AWAY OR FACILITATION?

Many school board members and/or district-level leaders might be wondering, "If we give greater responsibility to schools to govern themselves, won't the need for our positions fade away?" Interestingly enough, while we believe that giving greater autonomy to educators at the building level might cause *managerial* decisions to fade away, it actually requires a greater facilitation of *leadership* to plan for, review, and implement school renewal. Fewer bureaucratic decisions will need to be made at the central office, likely leading to a reduction in some central office personnel. However, those that stay will be tasked with three important tasks, namely: 1) Helping schools stay focused on instructional issues and quality learning experiences; 2) coordinating and sharing school renewal processes across the district and across other districts to facilitate organizational learning; and 3) providing and identifying resources for schools to address the work they cannot do themselves. The shift away from management, control, and power toward leadership that inspires, mobilizes, and rethinks our PK–12 educational system is crucial to the future of America.

ISSUES IN DEVELOPING DISTRICT POLICIES

When thinking about the resolve that is needed to develop district plans for school renewal, there are several important issues that need to be considered and addressed. In doing so, school boards and district-level leaders can play an important role in clarifying the responsibilities of educators throughout the entire district, as well as have game plans for when it is appropriate for the district to intervene and help address the affairs of individual schools. These issues revolve around vision and mission, decisionmaking protocols addressing control, communication structures around gray areas and what to do when these undefined issues arise, and commitment and responsibilities of the school district more broadly to ensure democratic self-governance has a chance to take hold and thrive in the long term.

Issue #1: Collective Vision and Mission of the District

Perhaps of greatest importance for district-level leadership is the need to help address the collective vision and mission of the district. What does the district stand for? Who has had the opportunity to provide input into developing the vision and mission? How are decisions made that directly affect teaching and learning? In what ways does the district support the internal self-reflection of practices to better meet the needs of a community? These questions (and more) address the promise, the pledge, and the problem-solving process through action research. In thinking about supporting democratic principles and self-governance, district leaders need to understand their role in facilitating decisionmaking processes, as well as the impact of what it means to say, "This is a district decision." Is there an established protocol when all voices are heard? When does a superintendent decide to make a unilateral decision? How is the school board brought into these decisionmaking processes? Why is it important to bring in representation that fully represents the school community and the larger community more broadly? Who is allowed influence in these protocols, and how is a council utilized in making decisions that promote democratic principles? These questions and more need to be given ongoing thought in developing a renewed vision and mission of the district.

Issue #2: What Schools Clearly Control

In redeveloping and reengaging the collective vision and mission of a district, there will be clear decisions that schools can and should be allowed to make on their own. These decisionmaking processes will naturally evolve over time, but inherently they should belong to individual schools and should not need to ask permission from the district. The school, rather, has the responsibility to serve the community to which it belongs, and in doing so keep the district informed of their decisions (revisit Chapter 3 for more information about this process). All constituents must understand that schools belong to the community, and decisions such as parental programing, scheduling, curriculum implementation, budgeting, staff development, teacher evaluation, and so on, remain at the building level if we are to support democratic ideals of school renewal.

Issue #3: What Districts Clearly Control

Of course, there are also decisions that will need to be made at the district level that cannot be made by schools. These decisions help to ensure that there is continuity about what the district offers in terms of the needs of the broader community the district serves. What are the decisions that cannot be made at the building level that impact all students, such as transportation, equitable maintenance and care about buildings and addressing student inequities, and allocation of resources to ensure local democratic principles can thrive? These decisions and points of facilitation to ensure school renewals for *all* schools within a district are equally crucial to the health of the learning organization.

Issue #4: Communication Structures to Address Gray Areas

As much as school districts might try to plan and develop protocols for decisionmaking processes around school renewal, there will always be gray areas that arise. When this occurs, the district should maintain control over the gray areas until a communication structure can be established to address the issue in question. Once the communication structure around the issue has been established, schools can request a waiver to move the decisionmaking process to the building level as long as the agreed-upon givens meet the vision and mission of the district. How does the school plan on gathering input from stakeholders to ensure the decision is welcomed at the building level and is supported by parents of the students the building serves? How does the district help ensure a reflective process is used to enact equitable treatment of students? In what ways will the decisions made at the building level further support community development, and what supports are needed from the district to help monitor implementation? These questions should focus on how the district might better support and empower buildings to address inequitable practices at the building level.

Issue #5: Commitments and Responsibilities of a District to Support Democracy and Self-Governance

When making the decision to support school renewal, district leadership transitions away from power and control and shifts toward moral leadership considerations. What are the commitments required of district leaders to provide structure and support for increased democratic self-governance? What are the inherent responsibilities of district leadership to focus on program development that will provide a school system capable of meeting the needs of developing citizens, who as a result, are able to influence our society in the 21st century? How and in what ways might district leaders guide and mentor schools by facilitating reflective practices that move a school away from standardized accountability structures toward rethinking the American PK–12 public school system to be more accountable to the local community? This is perhaps the most critical issue to address for district-level leaders who are committed to the school renewal process.

THE MORALITY OF DECENTRALIZATION

In order to help schools focus on accountability at the community level and to address student learning that directly contributes to increased democracy throughout our country, district policies must focus on the primary purpose of educating students to be productive and active citizens. District policy, at best, facilitates school–community partnerships to support moral development of self-governing structures and engagement of students. At worst, district policy obstructs teachers and community members from addressing local issues and forces educators and parents to comply with an education system that they regard as immoral and oppressive. After nearly 20 years of failed accountability efforts at the national and state level, there is a moral dimension of locally organized and governed schools where citizens should be directly involved in helping decide what is right and reimagining a school system that is morally compelling.

When a district is cognizant of the leadership required to promote the moral work of school renewal, it actively works with schools and the communities they serve to decentralize decisions previously made at the district level. However, this shift can often create confusion and frustration in the community as a power vacuum forms when power is shifted from the district level to the building level. When a school chooses to become more democratic and take greater control for its own accountability, it also chooses to accept greater responsibility for its actions, and in doing so the district should make every effort not to interfere when controversy arises. Often, this is easier said than done, and it can lead to difficult lessons for schools and districts as they move further toward school renewal. Change is hard for educators within a single school district, but it can be just as hard for community members who might attempt to leverage political clout to prevent decentralized school improvement efforts.

As a district transitions through the school renewal process, district leaders need to fight the impulse to keep schools as they are through the power structure of centralized authority. New work, based on responsible, school-based renewal, will inevitably spark some sort of public controversy. Instead of taking the matter over and deciding the political issue for themselves, district leaders need to signal support for building leaders to make decisions and to keep responsibility at the building level where community members and school-based educators determine solutions collaboratively and together. When a district signals that a school has the power and control to make a decision that impacts the instruction, learning, and use of physical space within a building, it is also stating that repercussions belong to the school as well. As a result, it is not the job of the school board or the superintendent to resolve or negotiate the solution, but rather it is the moral responsibility of the school and community members to which the school belongs to find common ground. Again, in this realigned role, school boards and district-level leaders help schools by reflecting on their actions and considering the best steps forward to engaging a community in the learning and teaching that will best serve the future citizens of our country.

Of course, not all issues will unfold simply or be resolved clearly. Some will even persist for quite a long time. The ongoing dilemma for school boards and district-level leaders will be to answer this simple question: "Do I really want to give schools responsibility to make their own decisions, and do I believe that by empowering them to make decisions at the building level the community will be better served?" The politically expedient thing to do is to control schools through policy—but we've seen how that experiment has played out in real time. The moral thing to do is to develop policies that will promote teaching and learning that can be directly applied to improving communities by addressing pressing issues. Anything less than that takes the school renewal process off course.

Part III

MOVING BEYOND IDEAS AND INTO ACTION

CHAPTER 9

Dilemmas of Good Schools
Pinpointing and Moving On

Jerome Bruner, the eminent educator, once said that education is an endeavor of learning how to manage dilemmas, rather than how to solve problems. Those who live or work in the day-to-day life of schools know what he meant. Problems, once identified or properly diagnosed, have solutions that can be applied, and then the problems are gone. Dilemmas, by contrast, are troublesome situations of tension, trade-offs, and competing consequences, no matter what the solution. School renewal is not a straight line of solving one problem after another until all the hurdles are crossed and the finish line is reached. Educational renewal means managing a stream of predicaments and learning to live with competing consequences, so that, over time, the school comes closer to realizing its goals for students.

As we saw in the previous chapter, if a school takes the initiative in school renewal, it is most likely to increase conflict among participants and receive additional criticism from outsiders. Thus, in solving one problem—becoming more democratic—the school creates two additional ones: internal conflict and external scorn. What seemed at first glance like the solution to a problem is really a dilemma; one apparent solution creates further tension to be resolved. This is life in a self-renewing school. To believe that a purposeful and moral school can operate without dilemmas and tension, and that a finished state of utopia can be reached, is delusionary, at least, if not downright psychotic. A good school is constantly seeking and creating new dilemmas for itself, as part of its own learning process.

THE ISSUE OF TIME

On hundreds of occasions, when we have spoken to members of individual schools and districts about school renewal, the question of time has been brought up. There is no single clear solution. A few commonsense ideas, from rudimentary to complex ones, will be suggested here in the form of questions.

1. Could existing planning days, as well as existing faculty meetings, be reconstructed to offer more time for planning in school renewal?
2. Is there a way of acquiring additional planning time for some members by rescheduling the school day, so that there can be occasional early-release time for the governing council or a task force?
3. Could existing money for staff development be used for school retreats or special planning sessions? Could additional money for planning be sought from the district, the state, or granting agencies?
4. Could or should stipends be given to school community members who have extraordinary responsibilities for the governance process? For example, some schools routinely give stipends to members involved in extracurricular activities. Could the same be done for the chairperson of the school council or for some other positions?
5. Is there an existing planning process, required by the district, the state, or an accrediting agency, that has to be conducted anyway and could become part of planning for the promise, the pledge, and the problem-solving process?

A school must strike a balance between the time people are willing to give to a schoolwide democratic process and the time individuals must devote to their classrooms, families, and personal affairs. For example, dedicated teachers typically want to participate in school renewal, but they do not want to be absent from their classrooms for long periods. Even if the time is used for planning ways of better education for all children, each day away from the classroom is a day lost forever to one's own students. The basic solution to the issue of time is not to solve it. Instead, school community members themselves must be able to decide how much time can be realistically and willingly devoted to this process and what can be done within that time—the greatest priorities within the given time. There are no set solutions. Experience with many schools shows that some find much time and others move ahead slowly, with less time allocated. When teachers have more say about the time (how much and when) they devote to school roles and responsibilities, they are more likely to do it willingly. Resentment results when others dictate teachers' time. The point, for any school, is to get started and then adjust expenditures of time as the years unfold, increasing or decreasing the time according to the will of the community. A shortage of time should never be an excuse for doing nothing.

EXTERNAL REGULATIONS

Policies must be developed that invite willing schools to move beyond existing regulations, within clear parameters, and that keep regulations temporarily in place for schools not yet ready to initiate their own school-wide changes. Some schools and districts may be ready to go beyond current regulations, but higher authorities are not ready to rethink them. After more than a decade of "legislated learning," most schools and districts are still subjected to uniform regulations of student assessment, curriculum, teacher evaluation, and more. It is also not uncommon to find local schools tightly controlled by uniform requirements of their own districts that are more restrictive than state and federal decrees. For schools and districts ready for democratic self-renewal but caught in a web of top-down regulations, the following guidance may prove helpful:

1. Study existing regulations, and determine which ones are actually helpful or at least will not get in the way.
2. Identify any regulations that truly are immediate barriers. Keep in mind what the school could still do even if the regulations did not change. For example, if the student testing program or the graduation requirements cannot be changed, what other student assessments or activities for graduation could still be performed in a way that would help achieve the primary school goal? A school should not let existing regulations be a reason for not taking at least some self-initiated steps.
3. If an invitational policy for seeking waivers from district or state regulations does not exist, initiate your own requests for waivers. Target the precise regulations standing in the way and prepare a short letter of inquiry, a paper, or an oral presentation to the appropriate authority. A school should have done its homework in making a request, which will state the goal, the intended results, the desired operations (after a review of literature and research), and the needed waiver. The request should have endorsements indicating wide school community support.
4. Press for the development of new policies at the district, state, and federal levels to encourage and invite site-based autonomy. Many state boards of education and school districts have developed such policies, some of which came out of the proposal process for charter schools, both public and private.
5. If testing requirements can't be changed, another internal question might be: In what ways can pressure on teachers related to standardized testing be lessened or alleviated so that we can still move ahead with democratic practices?

Individual schools usually have the capacity to move more quickly in making internal changes than external authorities can in responding. When a school wants to initiate, but the district or state has no policy or known procedure for giving waivers to schools, tension is the result. A school cannot simply wait, immobilized, but it also cannot simply act on its own, in a manner that is in clear noncompliance with district and state regulations. In such circumstances, during the transition prior to articulation of a new district policy, a school needs to ask openly for external approval. If that is not forthcoming, the school still needs to press ahead with internal change that stays within the letter of the law but finds enough flexibility for the school to act consistently with its principles. This is when it is important for principals to express support for teachers and reduce pressure related to accountability measures. This is a tough dilemma that can be entirely resolved in the future. For now, it must be discussed openly, and communication must be kept flowing among initiating schools, the district, and the state.

VOICE

Voice means influence and control over decisions. The school-based renewal movement should not exclude representatives of teachers' unions and associations, district officials, superintendents, school board members, business or civic groups, and others from matters of educational practice at the school level. Nevertheless, school renewal should rest squarely on the shoulders of those closest to teaching and learning—teachers, school-based administrators, staff, parents, and students themselves. Within this circle, what groups should have the greatest representation and voice in decision-making? There must be a clear rationale for why one group should have a greater voice than others.

One of us attended a meeting of various task forces dealing with how to improve an entire community in one of the highest-poverty and highest-crime areas of a large city. The participants were there to decide on ways to improve education, safety, employment, housing, and the general health and well-being of the community. Local citizens comprised the majority of the participants, but there were also officials from hospitals, banks, the police department, social service agencies, public schools, and others. It was clear that those officials, although they were *involved* in the community, were not *residents* of the community. They were there to provide information, insight, and suggestions and, *most of all*, to listen and respond to the *needs of the residents*. The residents were to have the majority influence in final decisions because no one knew better than the residents themselves what happens to them. This meeting, one in a series of meetings throughout high-poverty areas of this city, was an example of democracy at the local level, in the tradition of the old town meetings.

In a school community, the residents who live most intimately with the issues of schoolwide teaching and learning are teachers. Similarly, these "residents" should have the majority voice in those decisions. The principal should be a key participant (see Teacher Powered Schools, 2019). Parents and caretakers, students, paraprofessionals, district personnel, and civic or business leaders should be active members. District officials, however, should serve in a role similar to that of the officials at the town meeting: They should be resource people offering information, ideas, suggestions, and inside expertise on linking resources to the needs and ideas of residents developing programs.

This idea is sure to alienate some, but district officials, teachers' union or association representatives, parents, school administrators, and other groups should not have the majority influence or veto over decisions about teaching and learning in an individual school. Parents should have the majority say in parental matters. District officials should have the majority say in district matters. Teachers should have the majority say in teaching matters. There are two reasons why. One reason is obvious, and one is less so. The first reason is that decisions about teaching and learning affect teachers the most; they, more than anyone else in a school or district, must live with the consequences of those decisions in their day-to-day lives. The second reason is that teachers know more about teaching, potential changes, and likely consequences for students than anyone else does. Teachers, as the ones who possess experience and expertise, should have more say about schoolwide teaching matters than anyone else because *they have not left teaching.*

People who have become principals, union representatives, central office supervisors, or superintendents have given up their "residency" in the teaching community by leaving the classroom. This does not mean that such people and positions cannot be valuable participants and have a voice, but it does mean that they should not have majority control over local school decisions.

For school renewal to sustain itself, teaching has to come of age as a profession, and current assumptions about teachers and their influence on teaching matters must be reversed. It is ordinary for teachers to leave teaching and become principals, curriculum directors, superintendents, or union heads in order to have greater influence in education, or to have the time to make changes that cannot be made by teachers.

The absurdity and wrongness of this thinking holds schools back from realizing their potential. Why must teachers leave teaching in order to have a voice in changing teaching? Why should the benefits of time, flexibility, communication, visits with others, and (usually) higher salary accrue to those who leave teaching? Let us be blunt: The reason why teachers do not have more time, more flexibility, and more opportunities for professional dialogue is that our current system gives those benefits to people who leave teaching, rather than to those who stay.

Schools will never sustain school renewal until those who stay in teaching are rewarded by having the greatest influence over what happens in teaching and learning, and until those who leave teaching serve primarily as resources for teachers and their decisions. If you leave teaching, you lose your right to be a primary voice. This is a tough premise to swallow, and much ego, status, and power are at stake in keeping things the way they are; but a profession cannot exist in schools where teachers do not have the greatest say about the core work of teaching.

Such a change in dismantling hierarchies and dependency relations has occurred in some schools, has begun in others, and is being thought about in others, but this change will not come about if decentralizing initiatives to schools simply replace one level of management with another. Site-based schools run by lay citizens, management teams of administrators, appointed grade-level or departmental heads, or single principals are not the answer to self-renewal. Developmentally, teachers and administrators may not yet be willing to distribute, share, and take these responsibilities, and transitional stages toward democracy may be appropriate, but the end is clear.

Majority representation by teachers in decisions about teaching does not imply that a teacher alone should have a greater vote than any other school community member. To make good decisions for students, all members of the school community should be involved. The solution to the dilemma of voice has to do with where to begin with one's promise, pledge, and problem-solving process and whether to have all groups represented at once or to begin mainly with educators (teachers and administrators) and then expand representation of parents, students, and others over time.

COORDINATING WITH OTHER SCHOOLS

It is possible to construe site-based democratic school renewal as the unleashing of a hodge-podge of individual school initiatives that have no relation to what other schools in the same district or state are doing. The development of state and district invitational policies may be seen as creating an anarchy of individual school efforts. Exactly the opposite will occur, however, if districts and states provide support and link schools to one another. After the initial flurry of piloting efforts, there will be greater coordination of school efforts in implementation than now occurs under highly centralized and explicitly uniform regulations. The difference is that coordination will spring from the bottom up—from the interest of school people in learning from one another, and from the efforts of school people to ensure continuity of educational practice for their students as they move from school to school.

We have become so accustomed to thinking that the coordination of curricula, instructional programs, and assessment happens only by centralized fiat that we have forgotten that most successful coordination comes from people who want to discover ways of improving their practice by learning from and sharing with each other. For example, is cooperative learning, as an instructional practice, or the learning portfolio, as an assessment practice, better coordinated by a district or a state that determines the need, develops the idea, sets up training for schools, establishes schedules, provides training, and sends out monitors to assess the implementation? Or is it better coordinated and sustained when individual schools, through their own governance processes, decide on a need and join with like-minded schools in the district or state to work with resource people and learn to implement the effort jointly? Schools in comparable settings or spans of grade levels, using the critical-study dimension of the three-dimensional framework, may well be exploring some of the same changes; they will not want to reinvent the wheel. This may sound paradoxical, but it would be perfectly appropriate for schools to participate in district- or state-coordinated staff development programs, curriculum work, and other teaching-related practices when a need has arisen in multiple schools.

Does anyone truly believe that only district or state officials care that what a student learns in one school not be eradicated at the next level of schooling? Most primary, elementary, middle, and secondary school educators—on their own, and without prodding—care very much about what happens to their students. The dilemma in decentralized activities is how to coordinate the groundswell of individual school concern and save every school from the need to work and invent alone.

Schools that share students across levels will naturally want to know (and coordinate, to some degree) what they are doing. Coordination does not imply sameness of programs, but it does mean that each school understands the educational experiences and assessments provided by the others enough that it can build on them and prepare students for the next level. Again, this is where district personnel can serve another need, providing opportunities for schools to meet and be better informed about and coordinated with one another's work.

DEPENDENCE ON EXTERNAL AUTHORITIES

Knowingly or not, commercial publishers, staff development consultants and trainers, technology firms, and district and state officials have formed an alliance that has repeatedly diminished the ability of local educators to think critically and responsibly. The marketing of answers for schools has kept schools habitually dependent on external authorities. Layers of centralized positions, highly expensive consultants and educational programs, teacher and school effectiveness programs, commercial books, expensive technology, textbooks, and kits have claimed to virtually guarantee improved student learning and performance. This multimillion-dollar industry has generated high volumes of articles, presentations, books, and workshops, which produce an endless list of factors, components, dimensions, and elements that schools need, in the proper way, to be successful.

Most of these people have good intentions, not all by any means, to be helpful, but what they are doing, in their own advocacy of answers for others, is continuing the separation of teachers from decisions about teaching and diminishing the democratic capacity of a school for knowledge production and knowledge application. More often, school improvement or "restructuring" is done by states or districts. They "go shopping" to find the best-sounding innovation, program, or consultant and show local school people what to do. Members of the local school community are made to believe, or have internalized the belief, that educational change is the province of others.

We will never forget the principal of a fine middle school who called and asked for recommendations of a consultant to conduct a yearlong series of workshops on a literacy-based curriculum. Knowing the middle school, we were startled by her request. The school had three teachers with great expertise in this approach, and their classes were recognized as exemplary models of practice. I asked the principal whether the task force on staff development had thought of using the school's own faculty for the workshops. She paused and said, "No, it never occurred to us or to me to use our own. We just thought an outside expert would be better." In this question, the principal's pause, and the later deliberation of the task force, people in the school realized how often they had denied their own expertise and saw how they could acquire knowledge without relying on external authority.

No external educational authority—no matter how renowned or well researched—knows for sure what others should do. At best, what such persons or programs can do, if they are honest, is say what they think will work, under what conditions, on the basis of their own experiences. External programs, materials, consultants, and research can and should be considered and possibly used when a school makes its own decisions, but a school should look first for resources within. Only when there is no internal expertise or no obvious way to help people acquire it should a school look outside.

SEQUENCE, EMPHASIS, AND THE PACE OF EDUCATIONAL CHANGE

As Schön (1995) states, "problems are messy and confusing and incapable of technical solution." And school renewal is almost never sequential and requires solutions beyond a technical realm. Factors of readiness and different intervention points must be taken into account. For example, some sides of the three-dimensional framework, and some educational tasks within the framework, are easier to build than others. At one school, it may be better to develop the promise before the pledge. At another, it may be better to develop the problem-solving process and then develop the promise and the pledge. At another school, it may be more appropriate to develop the problem-solving process and then develop the promise and the pledge. At still another school, it may be best to do all three tasks at once.

Schools have different histories and constellations of people and personalities. Developing the promise at one school may be so boring that it deflates enthusiasm for further schoolwide work. Or a school may recently have written a mission statement for some requirement, which was felt to be a waste of time, and the promise may seem suspiciously similar. In such a school, one of the two other sides of the framework may spark more interest and willingness. In another school, however, creating the promise can be a highly energizing and satisfying endeavor that gives momentum to the building of the other two sides. This school may be a congenial one whose community has never tackled a collegial task of this magnitude, and it sounds exciting. Members may think that it makes sense to have everyone come together; talk across grades and departments; and, for the first time, try to figure out what learning should be about.

To sustain educational renewal, it is critical for a school to have the three-dimensional framework, but it need not be built in a particular order. The same holds true for the sequence of educational tasks. Some educational tasks—*the work of internal change*—are more accessible to planning and implementation than others. These tasks are what a school has under its control and can adjust, modify, or change in order to reach its core goal.

Which tasks to work on first, and the order of working on them, cannot be prescribed externally. One school may already have implemented top-quality, site-based staff development programs and may now wish to integrate that work into a new coaching process among teachers and administrators. Another school may be timid in trying to bring about instructional change through schoolwide staff development and coaching. A school's history of isolation and suspicion may make the idea of teachers opening their classroom doors to one another for observation and feedback too threatening; a more comfortable launching pad for collegial work may be curriculum development or the instructional budget. In developing plans for what should be taught and what materials should be purchased to support a new curriculum, people may come together more easily. They can then get to know each other better before addressing some of the other educational tasks.

Ideally, decisions about which tasks should be given greater emphasis, and when, should follow from schoolwide learning priorities. Which task, if changed, has the greatest likelihood to improve identified conditions for students? To take on a task that already has negative associations may set a school back, whereas it can move ahead on the realization of its priorities if, in the beginning, it takes on tasks that it feels neutral about, open to, or fairly comfortable with.

It would be wonderful if school renewal were as easy as textbooks, illustrations, and diagrams suggest. Fortunately, the process does not lend itself to prescriptions that override the individual context of the school. Knowing where to enter and what pace to assume is itself a process of making educated decisions about what is most likely to work now and lead to better work later on. A school discovers whether it has responded appropriately to this dilemma by taking action, studying the action, and determining whether the work is bringing the school together in achieving educational results for students. If it is not, the entry point may have been a mistake, and the school will have to rethink entry points, emphases, and tasks for the next round.

DYSFUNCTIONAL BEHAVIOR

What if a school does everything suggested in this book? Do the resisters, the complainers, the apathetic, and the whiners just suddenly become involved, enthused, committed, and wise? There will always be people who do not like or do not want to be involved, and who will try their hardest to subvert and squash the plans of a school. Such people exist right now in schools that are conventional, bureaucratic, hierarchical, and authoritarian, and they will exist in schools that are collegial, flexible, participatory, and democratic. They come from all positions, all experience levels, and all backgrounds. The pragmatic issue is not whether they exist but rather in which type of school there will be less dysfunctional behavior, and in which type of school there will be more pressure on dysfunctional people to "get with the program."

Over time, in truly democratic schools, there will be fewer dysfunctional persons than in nondemocratic schools. In schools where there is a push to include, listen to, and invite people to participate, there will be less apathy and fewer complaints. It will not happen overnight. It may take several years for people to believe that they really can make an equal contribution (or to choose not to). Truly democratic schools, by definition, will have more people contributing and less dysfunctional behavior because the responsibility for turning the behavior around rests with the entire school community rather than with one person in authority. Therefore, the pressure to change dysfunctional behavior is greater and more persuasive in democratic schools. A person who exhibits dysfunctional behavior, and the school community members who are the targets, spark a two-way responsibility for change.

In neo-conventional schools, the dysfunctional behavior of a school member is mainly an issue between the principal, who is responsible for the actions of her/his employees, and the dysfunctional person. The rest of the school members, besides rolling their eyes and exchanging the latest gossip about the battle going on between the two parties, mostly stay out of the issue. If they do feel a need to take sides, they tend to side with their colleague, rather than with the principal. But even taking sides usually means not helping the administration try to correct the problem.

In a democratic school, when a member is dysfunctional, he or she is out of compliance with what the school community has determined to be in the best interest of students and in accord with the school's promise for teaching and learning. Therefore, dysfunctional behavior is seen as going against the norms of the school community, rather than against the expectations of an employer. The dysfunctional person is interfering with what the school is trying to accomplish, and the school community needs to figure out how to correct the situation. When the school accepts the choice to act as a community, it also accepts responsibility for supervising itself and not passing such problems on to authority figures.

School community members need to be sensitive to the fact that complaining and resisting are normal human symptoms of feeling excluded or of not believing that one has been listened to or of believing that what is being done is not the right thing to do. All members, at some time, have exhibited the same dysfunctional behavior that they are seeing in someone who is obstructing the school's work. Therefore, the first step toward resolution is to analyze why one would act in the same way—in what circumstances, and for what reasons. Instead of seeing the behavior as symptomatic of the person's dysfunction, see it as a reflection of how the person has been included, communicated with, and treated by the group. For example, if dysfunctional behavior is characteristic of a small percentage of school members, it may be a signal that the school needs to work harder in learning how to listen and to include rather than finding ways to ignore, exclude, or blame the dysfunctional members.

Only by such reflective action can a school community determine whether the dysfunctional behavior is a result of poor involvement and communication or of lack of belief in what the school has decided to do. (Words that suggest a values-based stance of opposition are usually cast in the first person: "I am not going to change my teaching that way. I don't care what anyone else thinks, I'm not going to do it.") If it becomes apparent that the dysfunctional behavior is values based, then the next issue of democratic management lucks in: how to respect an individual's rights and still move forward as a school. If it acts too hastily, a community that has not weighed the opposition's views carefully may disregard important information. Expressions of disagreement are to be valued in the decisionmaking process, and the school should give all members ample opportunity to make the opposing case.

If push comes to shove, however, after the school community has listened, tried to be inclusive, considered alternatives, and deliberately made a schoolwide decision consistent with its promise and its decisionmaking process, then confrontation is inevitable. This is the hardest part of collective responsibility: A community must tell its own members that something was agreed on and is going to be done. Reluctant people can ask for help with accepting the implementation, but no one individual or group of individuals can stop what the group has legitimately decided.

This does not mean that a decision or a plan cannot be reconsidered later, after a trial period. Critical study of actions is part of the process. Nevertheless, a member must either act as part of the school or face the consequences. On several occasions, I have heard school community members confront their colleagues in words to this effect: "We want you here. You are entitled to your beliefs and expressions. But if you cannot accept the decision, then we would like you to consider taking a different position, where you will not be an obstacle to the work." These words are not easy and not nice. Many times, they are avoidable, but the world is not perfect. Dysfunctional behavior is the responsibility of everyone in a democratic school.

DILEMMAS AND DECISIONS

These dilemmas suggest that school renewal is always an educational process of making informed judgments about competing alternatives. The fact that there is no science or exact technology for school renewal reaffirms the central importance of analysis, insight, reason, and passion in the core work of education. If there is ever absolute precision in this work, then education as a process of thinking will have been lost, and there will be no reason for the existence of schools or democracies.

CHAPTER 10

Conclusion
If Not Now, Then When?

> The percentage of people who say it is "essential" to live in a liberal democracy is plummeting. . . . Support for autocratic alternatives to democracy is especially high among young people.
>
> —Jeffrey Rosen (2018)

The Hechinger Report (Chiles, 2018) noted that Revere High School, located in a working-class city with 80% of its students from low-income households and with 32 different languages spoken by recent immigrants, has dramatically improved academic achievement measured on multiple assessments in English, math, and science. Additionally, the graduation rate has jumped from 71% in 2009 to 87.9% in 2017. What caused such equitable gains across all student groups?

It happened because an astute principal who, with the support of his district, brought students, faculty, and other stakeholders into a process that turned traditional education on its head; he empowered those who worked and learned in his school. The faculty implemented student-centered learning by "giving the students a voice to another level." And the official school leaders encouraged and supported teachers to demonstrate student proficiency via performance assessments and to extend learning beyond the classroom walls. The school became a democratically infused center of learning for everyone.

Please hold these following thoughts in mind as we come to the conclusion of this book. The word "freedom" replaced the word "kingdom" after the successful American Revolution. The revolution was based on the belief that humans could govern themselves far better than could a single authority or an elite stratum of society. Thus, the free would rule the public domain ("free-dom") rather than a king ("king-dom"). What participants of a democratic society needed in order to govern themselves was a "common education." Public education was to be public not because it was to be publicly funded but because it would educate the public.

Horace Mann argued successfully for the first statewide system of public schools in the 1840s by explaining that schools would be the great equalizer of conditions, universally provided for poor and rich alike and nonsectarian, and such schools would develop members of society who could exercise free and deliberate choices (Cremin, 1964). Democracy and education were to be inseparable from each other. Democracy was as much an education theory as it was a political theory, a theory that people learn best through experiences, interchanges with others, and problem solving while respecting the dignity of all.

Public school educator and leader George Wood (2005) explained how his secondary public school in southwest Appalachia (Ohio) became an outstanding long-term example of education for democracy. He noted that the collective promise of this school was from its very beginning to educate students as wise citizens who would make good neighbors, think deeply and intelligently about issues of self and society, care for and respect others and take care of their family needs, and who would contribute to the welfare of others (also cited in Glickman, 2003). And such a promise had to be reflected in how classrooms were taught, how curriculum and staff development was used, and how students would graduate based on public demonstration of how they use their academic school knowledge to solve real-world issues. Twenty-plus years later the democratically infused high school continues on with a second generation of faculty, staff, and administrators.

Experts on workforce skills reaffirm the importance of democratic learning in an ever-shifting world. Jerry Useem (2019) in a featured article in *The Atlantic* reports on studies that underscore the importance of "'Psychological hardiness'—a construct that includes . . . a willingness to explore 'multiple response alternatives,' a tendency to 'see all experiences as interesting and meaningful,' and a strong sense of self confidence." As he further states, "Fluid, learning-intensive environments are going to require . . . things like ability to learn quickly from mistakes, use of trial and error, and comfort with ambiguity" (2019, p. 63).

HOW TO TAKE THIS BOOK AND RUN WITH IT

Our students have become increasingly alienated from participation as members of their larger society (Mehta & Fine, 2019) at the very time that we as a society need greater engagement and participation in order to reinvigorate democratic society. In most schools, learning has little relevance to becoming a citizen. Our students are not learning the essentials—how to care about, know about, and act for the betterment of the larger community. For a true awakening of our schools, we must return to their central goal: democratic participation. Other areas of achievement (in reading, writing, mathematics, art, and music) are more fully learned when they are viewed as subsets of student involvement in the core issues of local and expanded communities. To rejuvenate education, the public school itself needs to be a model of thoughtful and moral discourse (Levinson, 2014).

It does so by building and operating the three-dimensional framework. The first side is the promise: the agreed-upon principles of teaching and learning that the school community agrees to promote. The second side is the pledge: the agreed-upon and explicitly democratic process by which school community members acquire genuine power in making educational decisions. The third side is the problem-solving process, by which the school community gathers information and studies itself as it strives to achieve learning priorities. With the three-dimensional framework in place, the school community is ready to do the work of educational rejuvenation. That work includes such elements as schoolwide curriculum development, staff development, coaching, instructional programs, learning assessment, instructional materials, staffing, and scheduling. Over time, the school must determine a pace and a scope for change that will make it a qualitatively better place than before.

District and state policies must change to support the primary goal of public education and respect the developmental differences of schools. Such policies must not mandate uniformity and procedures. Rather, they must view fairness as enabling equality of accomplishment, not sameness of educational treatment. Policies must invite the school to move beyond existing regulations and use a site-based promise, a pledge, and a problem-solving process to craft a unique, powerful educational environment. If schools stay within the givens of constitutional law, equity, multicultural sensitivity, attention to research, progress toward achievement of learning goals, and public disclosure of results, then they should be actively encouraged to be as creative and imaginative as possible. The role of districts, boards, and state agencies becomes one of supporting schools by decentralizing resources, linking schools, providing technical and human assistance, and keeping access open to schools that are not yet ready to initiate school renewal.

An awakening of schools, districts, and states to the central democratic goal of schools will create confusion, controversy, and dilemmas—in sum, the peaks and valleys characteristic of emerging, free, moral communities. Such tensions should be expected, and clear policies for schools will serve as a stabilizer for the stormy weather ahead. In the end, what will have been achieved will be a school renewal movement that will endure because it will have a foundation not easily buffeted by fads, innovations, and shifting political winds. It will be secure as a true democracy is secure—in its constant openness and its inquiry into the larger questions of society. Renewal will endure, not because it will attain role maintenance, but rather because it will constantly be challenged. More thought, more study, more participation, and more action will be demanded.

This surely is not a perfect world, but it is a more moral world than we have now in our schools and in our society. School community members will not become wise, knowing, and effective all at once. A community has to learn as it goes—to learn from successes and, just as important, to learn from failures and crises. In a true community, wisdom is built over time and is based on cumulative experience. So, it will be in the rejuvenation of the public schools.

RESTRUCTURING POLICY

We must rethink policies for school change—invitations to willing schools; democratic use of funds; structures for schools and districts that are not ready; boards and state agencies as coordinators of the work of individual schools, rather than as enforcers of uniform compliance (see Appendix C). Those who have previously controlled schools, teachers, and teaching—districts, states, school boards, teacher unions, universities, consultants, and commercial publishers—will have to restructure themselves. Little in education and schools will change if those who have traditionally exercised control over teaching, teachers, and schools do not accept this premise: Those who leave the local school community lose the right to exercise dominative influence over decisions at the local site. If one has chosen to become a superintendent, a central office person, a university faculty member, or a board member, then one has intentionally removed oneself from the web of the local school community. The job of one who has left is to help those who have stayed and provide the time, resources, and assistance to judge for themselves what has to be done. The people who have stayed behind must learn to lead; those who have left must learn to follow.

The tradition of vesting authority for educational policies in external agencies, far removed from individual schools, must end. State commissions, governors' offices, national commissions, and national associations have served more to distract schools from their moral work than to help mobilize them in ways that will best help students learn. The only reforms that mean much are local reforms, in local schools and local communities. Local school community members have spent too much time reacting to state and national reports and external regulations and too little time developing their own ideas for their schools. We need to find more time for school communities to study themselves and get to work. Then and only then will we have an enduring national reform movement. The only national reform that will make much sense is a national reform made up of local reforms in the aggregate.

Conclusion

A SOBERING APPRAISAL OF THE NEED TO FOCUS

This book has dealt directly with the essential work of schools, but other influences that affect education are not under the primary control of local school communities. For example, there are dilapidated school buildings unfit for human occupancy, with inadequate heating and cooling systems, structural flaws, poor lighting, and general lack of maintenance. Our schools are infiltrated with the societal problems we all face, including drug use disorders, violence, and various forms of abuse. There are inadequate services for children living with little adult supervision and with few means of experiencing museums, libraries, and other institutions of historical, cultural, and aesthetic value. The list could go on to include teenage pregnancy, poor prenatal care, opioid epidemics, inadequate health care, and much more.

Our public schools contribute only a piece of what influences and educates students: the internal work of education. It is a significant piece but rarely does it deal with the external work of improving conditions in society. This distinction sets realistic limits on what a school community can do and helps to define the role of the other agencies and organizations with whom the school can collaborate. We shall direct the following statements primarily to educators in schools (principals, teachers, and paraprofessionals) and secondarily to other members of the school community (parents, caretakers, business and civic leaders, and other citizens):

1. The primary work of a public school community is to enhance the quality of teaching and learning within the school and to forge links to student learning outside the school.
2. The primary work of a public school community is not to spend time planning with respect to poverty, crime, health, social services, housing, and welfare.
3. The primary work of a public school community is a piece of the larger work of enhancing the total quality of a child's life.

Now, after stating this, we cringe at how it might be interpreted. Are we saying that a school community should be indifferent to these other issues? Not at all. We are saying that until schools understand the locus of control of their own responsibilities—teaching and learning—they will spend their time figuring out what other agencies should be doing and will forget or ignore what they themselves should be doing and why there are schools in the first place. To put this another way, teachers should not be spending most of their time planning lunch programs, maintaining their buildings, planning prenatal parenting programs, or providing additional psychological or social services. They should be spending most of their professional time discussing and planning for teaching and learning. It is up to others in the school community to determine connections with other agencies, to coordinate a wider spectrum of educational services. In the case of schools with deplorable physical conditions and striking inequality of resources, it is the moral obligation of districts and states to rectify those conditions.

Some of the most successful schools for impoverished students are strongly coordinated with other community services (Tough, 2008), but at the center of these schools is a strong promise for teaching and learning and a sense of the need to stay focused on the internal work of schoolwide educational practice. Some of the worst schools are those where internal practice is neglected, and the onus of responsibility for educating students is shifted to external parties. What this analysis means is that, for now, school renewal alone will not save our children from the life that they live after school. There will still be hunger, violence, neglect, and unspeakable tragedy. What school renewal will do is take children squarely from these outside conditions and educate them in the most profound, powerful, and purposeful way that a school community can imagine. If all other institutions would do likewise in dealing with their primary responsibilities and then link up with one another, we would have integrative care for our children, our communities, and our society at large. The total challenge is daunting, but to begin is to begin with oneself. If public education can engender in students a desire to participate as productive citizens in the larger society, then we will indeed have a better place for future generations.

BELIEVING

Schools, districts, and states that take up the challenge of creating local school renewal will find that day-to-day realities will continue to crop up and make immediate life unpredictable—sometimes crazy, always interesting. Influence outside the school will continue to seep in. Problems with logistics and schedules will continue. In the course of thousands of human interactions each day, some will be problematic. In the short term, the observable changes in a school beginning renewal may not be obvious. Classrooms, the curriculum, grouping, and teaching may appear to be only somewhat modified, and students may not seem much more productive, excited, or involved than before. School renewal is not a day-to-day proposition. It is a long-term, continuous proposition, and commitment must be for the long term.

In many cases, schools can expect to achieve modest improvements for students in the first year of renewal and will see more comprehensive and dramatic changes after 3, 4, or 5 years. These schools move to a rhythm of surges and lulls. At times, maintaining change is paramount. At other times, discarding existing routines is paramount. At all times, however, there is a clear purpose and direction to the work. The ultimate issue is staying the

Conclusion

course—believing that the work of a democratic school will benefit students and, eventually, society at large. The actions taken may not always be correct, but when results are not forthcoming, the school needs to alter its decisions and actions, not its belief in democratic principles. In this way, democracy in its three-dimensional educational framework—the promise, the pledge, and the problem-solving critical analysis—transcends the setbacks, crises, and transitions of community members.

The belief in democracy is the foundation of a society that millions of people throughout the world have given their lives to create, protect, and maintain. We must do the same in our schools. To return to their central mission of preparing democratic citizens, schools must be founded on the same bedrock belief. We need to strive for the same microcommunity in our schools that we as a people would wish to have as a macrocommunity in our society.

A teacher friend of ours, who works in a renowned democratic school, describes why his school has come so far in the past decade, with documented success in preparing its students: "The reason why our school continues to work is that, as a community, we won't let it not work. No matter how frustrated, angry, and impatient we feel at times with each other, we know that we will not stray from our belief about democracy and education. Every challenge will be met because there is no other acceptable way." What he is describing is the cycle built on a reasoned faith that belief in core democratic principles frames the operations and decisions that will produce similar beliefs, operations, and decisions in students. This in essence is our challenge.

APPENDIX A

Sample Pledge to Democratic Governance

This sample pledge to democratic schooling should be seen as a simple illustration of the points for a school to consider in developing its own pledge, not as a pledge to be imitated. There are multiple ways to govern democratically and many entry points. The following example is of governance with broad representation involving students, parents, the community, and the district. Many schools do not begin with such broad representation. Some schools use a final decision rule, going back to all members for approval.

PREAMBLE

It is our shared belief that we should maintain an emphasis on teaching and learning. Accountability and responsibility are two key words describing our democratic decisionmaking process. We strive to be open to new ideas and work through consensus or voting to arrive at decisions. Once group decisions are made, we all are expected to support them. Decisions are re-evaluated as necessary. It is our continual mission to develop school-renewal activities that meet the needs of all our students, not just for the benefit of one particular group.

CHARGE

We seek to uphold our school promise of teaching and learning principles through the following actions:

- To display concern for the total student and the needs of the school as a whole
- To foster an invitational and cooperative learning environment
- To be creative decisionmakers and problem solvers
- To communicate information systematically
- To develop internal leadership ability
- To be risk takers

- To stay informed
- To continuously evaluate our decisions, activities, and results for students

COMPOSITION OF THE SCHOOL COUNCIL

The council will consist of 14 voting members. Terms served on the council will be for a period of 3 years, with four or five positions available for election each year. A council member can succeed himself or herself if reelected. (Exception: The initial council will serve a 2-year term before the rotation process begins. Vacancies on the council are to be filled for unexpired terms by elected members from representative groups.)

- Administrative staff (principal): one standing member
- Classroom teachers, counselors, and specialists: seven elected members
- Representatives of parent organization: two elected members
- Representatives of student organization: two elected members
- Community/business partner: two elected members
- Other school staff personnel: two elected members
- District consultant: one ex-officio member

The school council will be responsible for the following tasks:

- Gathering information and ideas from all faculty, through the communication groups
- Establishing priorities for schoolwide improvements and organizing special task forces
- Making decisions on recommendations from the task forces
- Collecting and evaluating evidence of schoolwide improvement

Communication groups will consist of certified and noncertified staff members randomly allocated to each group. Each communication group will be led by an elected member of the council. Groups will meet monthly with their council representatives to disseminate information and to discuss concerns and ideas for schoolwide improvements. The parent and student representatives will use the parent and student organizations as their communication groups. Changes in the formation and assignment of members in communication groups will be made as members of the council changes.

Special task forces will be formed on the basis of schoolwide concerns for school renewal. Each task force chairperson (not a council member) will be responsible for making progress reports and recommendations in writing to the council. A recorder will be selected to take minutes of each meeting.

Minutes will be given to the vice chairperson of the council, who will serve as the liaison between the council and the task forces.

Standing committees will be determined by the council to deal primarily with nonteaching and nonlearning matters (student discipline, extracurricular activities, building maintenance, fundraising, coordination of social services, etc.). The composition of the committees will reflect representation of those most affected by the matters under discussion. Membership will include staff, parents, students, and community leaders.

LIMITATIONS OF GROUPS

The responsibilities of the school council and of school governance will be specific, will address schoolwide issues, and will focus on educational areas in need of improvement. The following areas will be restricted from consideration:

- Systemwide issues
- Personal or individual issues
- Issues in the realm of normal operational or organizational procedures (administrative or instructional) until a need for improvement has been identified by a communication group
- Issues at variance with established policies of local and state boards of education and other outside governing agencies

The focus will be on what we as a school community should do to better educate all our students.

MEETING SCHEDULES

The school council will meet at least once a month, and more often if necessary. For the purpose of decisionmaking, eight members will be considered a quorum. The following are protocol for when groups/committees will meet:

- Communication groups will meet monthly, and more often if necessary.
- Task forces will meet for the first time as scheduled by the vice chairperson of the council. After the initial meeting, they will determine their own schedule of meetings, based on convenient times for members and the number of meetings deemed necessary to accomplish the group's specific task.
- Standing committees will determine their own schedule for meetings, normally at least once a quarter. All meetings are open to all members of the school community.

DECISIONMAKING PROCEDURES OF THE COUNCIL

Concerns submitted to the council that are not within the parameters of shared governance will be referred to the appropriate group or individual. The following procedures have been established for the decisionmaking process:

1. Task force chairperson submits recommendations in writing to the council.
2. The council reviews, revises, accepts, or rejects the recommendation by consensus. For the purpose of this council, consensus will mean agreement of all members present.
3. If the council does not reach consensus on a decision, representatives return to their communication groups for additional feedback.
4. The council meets a second time, to try to reach consensus.
5. If consensus at the second meeting is still not forthcoming, recommendations are returned to the task force for reevaluation.
6. Recommendations from the task force's chairperson are resubmitted to the council.
7. A two-thirds majority of the council will suffice for a final decision in the event that consensus cannot be reached.
8. If there is not a two-thirds majority, no action is to be taken.

JOB DESCRIPTIONS

Chairperson

A chairperson sets the agenda for council meetings and schedules meetings. She/He conducts council meetings by doing the following:

- Stating objective(s) of meeting
- Reviewing agenda
- Outlining procedures for reaching decisions
- Facilitating communication among council members
- Summarizing decisions
- Sets agenda for future meetings and communicates with the group/committee

Vice Chairperson

A vice chairperson assumes duties of chairperson in chairperson's absence. She/He assists the chairperson in planning council meetings if assistance is requested. The vice chairperson also assumes duties assigned by the chairperson in conducting meetings and making presentations. She/He serves as the liaison between the council and task forces by doing the following:

- Scheduling the first meeting of the task force
- Supervising the selection of a task force chairperson and recorder
- Providing the recorder with the forms necessary to document task force business
- Scheduling the task force presentation to the council
- Filing task force reports

Recorder

The recorder supports the functioning of the group/committee by:

- Recording decisions reached by council
- Recording permanent data, such as committee assignments, schedule of next meeting, and so forth
- Maintaining or arranging maintenance of file containing all council business
- Keeping minutes of meetings and circulating to all school–community members

Communication Group Leader

The communication group leader supports the functioning of the group/committee by:

- Conducting communication group meetings
- Gathering and reporting information, concerns, and ideas of the group to the council
- Informing communication group of activities and decisions of the council

Task Force Chairperson

The task force chairperson supports the functioning of the group/committee by:

- Setting agendas and conducting task force meetings
- Reporting on progress of task force to the council
- Presenting task force recommendations to the council for decision

Task Force Recorder

The task force recorder supports the functioning of the group/committee by:

- Taking attendance at task force meetings
- Keeping minutes of task force meetings
- Completing task force record-keeping forms and giving them to council vice chairperson at conclusion of the task force's work

APPENDIX B

The Peakview School Pledge

MAKING A RADICAL COMMITMENT TO CONSENSUS: DECISIONMAKING AT PEAKVIEW

Early in the life of Peakview, when it was still in the conceptual stages, a style or approach to decisionmaking evolved that has become a hallmark of the way we work together. The underlying belief is that no one person holds all the truth. This basic assumption calls for us to value and respect the wisdom of each member of the staff while continuing to value the insight that we each have gained from our individual experiences and reflection.

In practical terms, it means that:*

1. Everyone has the opportunity and responsibility of initiating and then leading the group in the direction of a decision that needs to be made.
2. We all have the responsibility of speaking our minds, so that we all benefit from thinking of each other, but accepting the responsibility to speak implies accepting the responsibility to listen.
3. When our decisions are based on our collective priorities, we will do our best work, and when time is provided for both discussion and reflection, our decisions will more often be good ones.

We also have become attached to another notion: the distinction between "matters of preference" and "matters of conscience." As in all groups that struggle to do important work, we come to points when differing opinions and even differing philosophies raise the specter of real conflict. We are convinced that on the important issues we will thrive when consensus is reached. However, we have had the experience of reaching for closure on a decision only to find that one or two people remain opposed to the general drift of the large group. It is in those moments that the test of preference versus conscience is applied. If, after careful thought, a dissenting school community member is asked if the personal stand is one of preference, and

---

*The process is an adaptation of the Quaker meeting based on the previous work of Peakview School in Aurora, Colorado, and described in Glickman (1993).

the answer is yes, then that individual is expected to lay personal preference aside in order to allow the staff to move forward. If, however, the personal stand is a matter of conscience, then the community member assumes that the decision that was in the offing needs to be either delayed or abandoned.

On more than one occasion, we have found agreement and then, on the reflection of a single member, have had to reopen discussion and undo a decision, so that conscience could be followed. We also have had the experience of having consensus falsely identified, and the next day it took the courage of a single member to point out that what was heard was not, in fact, what was said.

As all school communities do, we struggle to find the balance between adequate discussion and thought on an issue and the need to get on with the work of the school through closure of a discussion. We are willing to press ourselves for good decisions, but we also allow and honor the temporary and incomplete decisions that we are sometimes forced to make when we lack the time, energy, or insight to bring a decision to its proper conclusion.

One strategy for decisionmaking that has served us well is the decision to operate as a committee of the whole. Our size (we are a relatively small school) has served us well in this regard. However, even in a relatively small community, this structure, combined with our commitment to real consensus, makes for a decisionmaking process that is cumbersome and time consuming, but the corresponding benefits have been clear to us—collectively, we have not made many poor decisions.

While we do not do this perfectly, we value a school culture that allows trust and honesty to prevail in an atmosphere of safety. None of our best efforts at working together would mean much without our fundamental caring for and about one another.

APPENDIX C

A Sample of a Process for Decentralizing Authority to Local Schools by a District and State Invitational Policy

SCHOOLS FOR THE FUTURE: PROGRAM GUIDELINES

Schools are encouraged to renew local education to accomplish local, state, and national education goals. The intent of this program is to encourage staff members of individual schools, with the support of local districts, to design the best education programs they can to improve the learning of their own students. It will assist and support schools, districts, and communities in being innovative, creative, and responsible for new approaches to educating students. Local and state rules, regulations, and standards that inhibit proposed restructuring activities will be waived according to the applicable statute.

DEMONSTRATION SCHOOLS

School renewal efforts should do the following:

- Focus on student learning as the end result
- Develop a new conceptualization of learning and teaching
- Engage students in a "thinking curriculum" rich in problem solving, analysis, synthesis, and other thinking skills
- Expect high levels of educational attainment of all students
- Focus on learners, not on perpetuating institutions or systems
- Share decisionmaking authority so that those responsible for carrying out decisions participate in making them
- Address local, state, and national goals

The program is designed to encourage these tasks:

1. The establishment of measurable goals for educational attainment and high expectations for student performance, including but not limited to improvement in the following performance measures:
    a. Student expectations and attitudes about learning
    b. Student success in lifelong learning
    c. Student attendance rates
    d. High school completion rates
    e. District, state, and national assessments of student learning and educational progress
    f. Parental involvement in school activities
    g. Student conduct
2. The restructuring of school organizations, school operations, curriculum, instructional approaches, roles of educators, and formal relationships between and among students, teachers, administrators, parents, and the community, including but not limited to the following modifications:
    a. Curriculum
    b. Delivery of instruction
    c. Assessment of student learning
    d. Graduation and promotion requirements
    e. Length and structure of the school day and the school year
    f. Staffing and formal roles and responsibilities of teachers, administrators, and other school personnel
    g. Personnel evaluation and staff development
    h. State rules, regulations, and standards, as well as local policies related to educational practices
    i. Formal and informal relationships between school districts and other entities, including community colleges, 4-year colleges and universities, businesses, social service agencies, and other institutions

Eligibility

The following schools, with the support of their superintendents and local boards, are eligible to apply:

1. New schools
2. Existing schools that (1) were in compliance on the most recent evaluation, (2) have previously initiated site-based improvement, and (3) are willing to attempt more creative and responsible educational changes.

Appendix C

Application Procedures

An application must be initiated at the school level. It must be supported by the principal and 80% of the teaching staff. The superintendent of schools and the local school board of education must approve the application.

The application process consists of two phases. The school must submit a letter of intent, to be followed by a full application. For a district that wants to open a new school, the application process should be initiated by the principal of the new school and the school's initial community council and coordinated with district personnel until the new school is staffed. At this point, the application process will become the responsibility of the principal and staff of the new school. Schools may submit letters of intent or applications at any time.

Applications may be approved for an initial period of up to 3 years. All accepted schools will submit yearly evaluations and receive on-site visits. If a school demonstrates success, a 3-year renewal of the application may be issued.

The letter of intent should indicate the school's intention to file a full application. The letter should briefly describe what the school staff has done to plan for restructuring, as well as any planning that remains to be done. It should describe the history of the school's involvement in a site-based improvement process, describe the nature of the school's anticipated renewal, and outline proposed activities. After the letter has been filed, the applicant will be contacted about whether the proposal is consistent with the intent of the program. The department will help local schools and districts obtain technical assistance to develop their applications.

The application should be developed in a form (written, video, audio, computer generated, visual, multimedia, etc.) and at a length decided by the applicant school. An application cover sheet and a one-page abstract describing the project must be in written form. The application must include the following:

- Identification of the decisionmaking group, committee, or council in the school and of the shared decisionmaking procedures for carrying out the overall plan
- The overall goals to be achieved by the restructuring
- The student learning and educational outcomes to be attained
- The major activities of the project, including but not limited to the nature and extent of the restructuring and timelines
- A description of staff development activities required to implement the planned restructuring
- A design for evaluating the effectiveness of the restructuring, including a projection of annual progress on indicators established by the school

- A written statement that district and school administrators are willing to exempt the school from local rules if modification or waiver of local school district rules is required
- Identification of and brief rationale for all state rules, standards, and regulations for which waivers or modifications are requested
- Written statements of support from parents, community agencies, local businesses, and other interested individuals and organizations, if available

Application Review

A committee will be appointed by the superintendent of schools. The committee will reflect a balance of local educators (teachers and building and district administrators), local school board members, Department of Education representatives, and others familiar with school renewal and evaluation. These may include college and university faculty, as well as business and community leaders. Committee members will serve on a rotating basis. The Department of Education will provide staff support for the committee.

The committee will review all letters of intent and all applications and will make recommendations about applications to the state board, through the state superintendent. The board will consider the recommendations of the committee quarterly and will make final decisions about approval of applications.

References

Benjamin, H. (1939). *The saber-tooth curriculum.* New York, NY: McGraw-Hill.
Blount, J. M. (2013). Educational leadership through equity, diversity, and social justice and educational leadership for the privilege imperative. In L. C. Tillman & J. J. Scheurich (Eds.), *Handbook of research on educational leadership for equity and diversity* (pp. 7–21). New York, NY: Routledge.
Breidenstein, A., Fahey, K., Glickman, C., & Hensley, F. (2012). *Leading for powerful learning: A guide for instructional leaders.* New York, NY: Teachers College Press.
Cheema, J. R., & Galluzzo, G. (2013). Analyzing the gender gap in math achievement: Evidence from a large-scale US sample. *Research in Education, 90*(1), 96–112.
Chiles, N. (2018). Teaching to the student, not the test. *The Hechinger Report.* Retrieved from hechingerreport.org/teaching-to-the-student-not-the-test
Cremin, L. (1964). *The transformation of the school: Progressivism in American education 1876–1957.* New York, NY: Vintage.
Datnow, A. (2011). Collaboration and contrived collegiality: Revisiting Hargreaves in the age of accountability. *Journal of Educational Change, 12*(2), 147–158.
Dewey, J. (1916). *Democracy and education: An introduction to the philosophy of education.* New York, NY: Macmillan.
Doddington, C. (2018). Democracy and education: Is it relevant now? *Education, 46*(4), 381–384.
Drago-Severson, E. (2009). *Leading adult learning: Supporting adult development in our schools.* Thousand Oaks, CA: Corwin.
Every Student Succeeds Act (ESSA). (2015). Pub. L. No. 114-95 § 114 Stat. 1177 (2015–2016).
Fahey, K., Breidenstein, A., Ippolito, J., & Hensley, F. (2019). *An uncommon theory of school change.* New York, NY: Teachers College Press.
Fair Test. (2019). Graduation test update: States that recently eliminated or scaled back high school exit exams. Retrieved from fairtest.org/graduation-test-update-states-recently-eliminated
Fullan, M. (2016). Developing humanity: Education's emerging role. *Principal Connections, 20*(2), 10–12.
Glass, T. E. (2000). Where are all the women superintendents? *School Administrator, 57,* 22–27.
Glazer, J. L. (2009). How external interveners leverage large-scale change: The case of America's Choice, 1998–2003. *Educational Evaluation and Policy Analysis, 31,* 269–297.

Glickman, C. D. (2003). *Holding sacred ground: Courageous leadership for democratic schools.* San Francisco, CA: Jossey-Bass.

Glickman, C. D., Allen, L., & Lunsford, B. (1994). Factors affecting school change. *Journal of Staff Development, 15*(4), 38–41.

Glickman, C. D., Gordon, S. P., & Ross-Gordon, J. M. (2018). *SuperVision and instructional leadership: A developmental approach* (11th ed.). Boston, MA: Allyn & Bacon.

Glickman, C. D., & Thompson, K. (2009). Tipping the tipping point: Public engagement, education, and service learning. Voices from the middle. *Journal of the National Council of English, 17*(1), 9–15.

Goleman, D., Boyatzis, R., & McKee, A. (2013). *Primal leadership: Unleashing the power of emotional intelligence.* Boston, MA: Harvard Business Review.

Grammatikopoulos, V. (2012). Integrating program theory and systems-based procedures in program evaluation: A dynamic approach to evaluate educational programs. *Educational Research and Evaluation, 18*(1), 53–64.

Gruenert, S., & Whitaker, T. (2015). *School culture rewired: How to define, assess, and transform it.* Alexandria, VA: Association for Supervision and Curriculum Development.

Guajardo, M. A., Guajardo, F., Janson, C., & Militello, M. (2016). *Reframing community partnerships in education: Uniting the power of place and wisdom of people.* New York, NY: Routledge.

Hanauer, N. (2019, July). Better schools won't fix America. *The Atlantic.*

Hargreaves, A. (1994). *Changing teachers, changing times: Teachers' work and culture in the postmodern age.* New York, NY: Teachers College Press.

Hess, F. M., & McShane, M. Q. (2019). The happy (and not so happy) accidents of Bush-Obama school reform. *Kappan, 100*(4), 33–39.

Hill, N. E. (2019, Winter). Good schools close to home. *Harvard Ed. Magazine.* Retrieved from gse.harvard.edu/news/ed/19/01/good-schools-close-home

Hutchens, D. (1999). *Shadows of the Neanderthal: Illuminating the beliefs that limit our organizations.* Waltham, MA: Pegasus.

Johnson, D. W., & Johnson, F. P. (2017). *Joining together: Group theory and group skills* (12th ed.). Boston, MA: Pearson.

Kegan, R., & Lahey, L. L. (2016). *An everyone culture: Becoming a deliberately developmental organization.* Boston, MA: Harvard Business School Publishing.

Knight, J. (2016). *Better conversations: Coaching ourselves and each other to be more credible, caring, and connected.* Thousand Oaks, CA: Corwin.

Levinson, M. (2014). *No citizen left behind.* Cambridge, MA: Harvard University Press.

Loewus, L. (2017). The nation's teaching force is still mostly white and female. *Education Week, 37*(1), 11.

McDonald, J. P. (2019). Toward more effective data use in teaching. *Kappan, 100*(6), 50–54.

Mehta, J., & Fine, S. (2019, March 29). High school doesn't have to be boring. *The New York Times.* Retrieved from nytimes.com/2019/03/30/opinion/sunday/fix-high-school-education.html

Meier, D., & Gasoi, E. (2017). *The schools belong to you and me: Why we can't afford to abandon our public schools.* Boston, MA: Beacon Press.

References

Mette, I. M., & Riegel, L. (2018). Supervision, systems thinking, and the impact of American school reform efforts on instructional leadership. *Journal of Cases in Educational Leadership, 21*(4), 34–51.

Meyer, H. D. (2009). Saying what we mean and meaning what we say: Unpacking the contingencies of decentralization. *American Journal of Evaluation, 115,* 457–474.

Morgan, G. (2006). *Images of organizations*. Thousand Oaks, CA: Sage.

National Center for Education Statistics (NCES). (2017a). *2017 digest of education statistics*. Retrieved from https://nces.ed.gov/pubs2018/2018070.pdf

National Center for Education Statistics (NCES). (2017b). Number and percentage distribution of public school principals by gender, race, and selected principal characteristics. Retrieved from https://nces.ed.gov/surveys/ntps/tables/Principal_raceXgender_Percentage&Count_toNCES_091317.asp

No Child Left Behind Act (NCLB) of 2001, P.L. 107–110, 20 U.S.C. § 6319 (2002).

Peck, C., & Reitzug, U. C. (2012). How existing business management concepts become school leadership fashions. *Educational Administration Quarterly, 48,* 347–381.

Rosen, J. (2018, October). America is living James Madison's nightmare. *The Atlantic*.

Santoro, D. A. (2018). Is it burnout? Or demoralization? *Educational Leadership, 75*(9), 10–15.

Schein, E. H. (2010). *Organizational culture and leadership* (4th ed.). San Francisco, CA: Jossey-Bass.

Schön, D. A. (1995). The new scholarship requires a new epistemology. *Change, 27*(6), 26–34.

Shields, C. M. (2014). The war on poverty must be won: Transformative leaders can make a difference. *International Journal of Educational Leadership and Management, 2*(2), 124–146.

Stiggins, R. J., Arter, J. A., Chappuis, J., & Chappuis, S. (2004). *Classroom assessment for learning: Doing it right—using it well*. Portland, OR: Assessment Training Institute.

Teacher Powered Schools. (2019). Collaborative leadership for thriving teams: A guide for teacher-powered site administrators. *A Project of Education Evolving*. Retrieved from https://www.teacherpowered.org/files/attachments/teacher-powered-administrators-guide.pdf

Tough, P. (2008). *Whatever it takes: Geoffrey Canada's quest to change Harlem and America*. New York, NY: First Mariner Books.

Useem, J. (2019, July). At work, expertise is falling out of favor. *The Atlantic*.

Wood, G. (2005). *Time to learn: How to create high schools that serve all students* (2nd ed.). Portsmouth, NH: Heinemann.

You, S., & Conley, S. (2015). Workplace predictors of secondary school teachers' intention to leave: An exploration of career stages. *Educational Management Administration & Leadership, 34,* 29–46.

Zdenek, R. O., & Walsh, D. (2017). *Navigating community development: Harnessing comparative advantages to create strategic partnerships*. New York, NY: Palgrave Macmillan.

Index

Page numbers followed by *f* and *t* indicate figures and tables, respectively.

Accountability, 1, 3, 30–31, 53, 55
   data source, 43, 43*t*, 44
   democratic governance, 45–46
   district policies, 98–99
   dysfunctional climate, 31
   external, 15
   measures, 24, 28, 31, 90
   regulated, 2
   unnecessary structures, 15
Accountability movement, 88–89
Actions. *See also* Dysfunctional behavior
   critical study, 114
   discretionary, 46
   reflective, 113
   research, 40–49, 90
Administrators, 13, 31
Adult learning, 17
Allen, L., 15
Allen, P., 2
Alternative education programs, 44
American Educational Research Association, 47
American Revolution, 115
Arter, J. A., 90
Assessments, 58–59, 90
Assumptions, 73
The Atlantic, 116
Authoritarian and transactional approach, 67, 68–69, 68*t*
Autocratic leadership, 88
Autocratic values, 17
Autonomy, 93

Benjamin, H., 40
Bill of Rights, 5
Black Lives Matter movement, 72
Blount, J. M., 12
Boyatzis, R., 13
Breidenstein, A., 15, 61, 62, 76, 86
Bruner, J., 103
Business management approaches to schools, 16

Change process, 66–67
   approaches used to, 67–69, 68*t*
   mental models, 66–67
Chappuis, J., 90
Chappuis, S., 90
Chiles, N., 115
Classes, messages about value of, 76–77
Closed systems, 69–70
Coaching. *See* Instructional coaching
Collegial schools, 18*t*, 19
Commitments of district, 98
Common schools, 5
Communication structures, 98
Communities
   developmental needs, 69–71
   engagement, 28–29, 30–31, 83–84
   schools making difference in, 73–74
   social needs, 2
Community-based action research, 40–49
   data sources, 42–44
   plan, 45, 45*t*
   questions, 41–42
Community-based learning projects, 44

Community–curricula connections, 77
Community Learning Exchange (CLE), 21
Competition vs. diversification, 80–82
Congenial schools, 18–19, 18t
Conley, S., 18
Constitution, 5
Constitutional law, 90
Control and power, 72
Cooperative learning, 109
Coordination, 108–109
Creative data source, 43, 43t, 44
Creative use of staffing, 78–79
Cremin, L., 116
Critical moments, 85–86
　addressing group dynamics, 85–86
　bridging gap between ideal and reality, 86
　losing to gain, 85
　organizational vulnerability, 86
Critical self-study process, 41
Critical study of actions, 114
Culture, 14, 27, 28t
Curriculum
　community connections, 77
　considerations and questions, 54–55
　description, 54
　development and implementation, 54–56
　prepackaged, 4, 16, 36, 47, 49, 55, 75

Data
　democratic governance, 45–46
　sources, 42–44, 43t
Datnow, A., 13
Decentralization, morality of, 98–100
Decisionmaking, 24–39.
　　See also Governance
　development, 25
　formality and procedures, 38–39
　frustration, 37–38
　guiding rules, 25–26
　locus of control, 26–27
　organizational patterns, 37
　overview, 24
　rules for governance, 29–31
Democracy, 116

Democratic approach, 67, 68, 68t, 69
Democratic schools, 25
　accountability data, 43
　considerations, 25
　de-privatizing instruction, 28
　dysfunctional behavior, 112, 113–114
　factors impacting, 27–29
　progressive data, 43–44
　sample pledge, 123–128
　as satisfying and rewarding place, 37
Demographics, 73
Departmental and grade-level teams, 64–65
Developmental needs, 69–71, 71t
Dewey, J., 15
Dialogue and conversations, 17
Dilemma, 103–114
　coordination, 108–109
　dysfunctional behavior, 112–114
　educational change, 110–112
　external authorities, 109–110
　overview, 103
　policies and regulations, 104–106
　voice and representation, 106–108
Direct participation, 34–35, 35f
Discretionary actions, 46
Districts
　boards and, 88–89
　collective vision and mission, 96–97
　commitments and responsibilities, 98
　communication structures, 98
　control, 97
　empowering schools, 89–91
　equality vs. equity, 91–92
　grant opportunities, 93
　issues in developing policies, 96–98
　leadership, 32, 96
　morality of decentralization, 98–100
　overview, 88
　plan for school renewal, 93–96
　resource allocation, 92
　role, 89
　seed money use, 92–93
　support maximizing democracy, 29
Diversification vs. competition, 80–82
Doddington, C., 14

Drago-Severson, E., 77
Dysfunctional behavior, 112–114

Education, 4–5
  books on, 47
  Bruner on, 103
  difficulties in changing current system, 15–17
  fragmented system, 24
  industrial model, 15–16
  infiltration, 16
  lack of professional dialogue, 17
  restricted thinking, 16–17
Educational priorities, 53–65
  curriculum development, 54–56
  departmental and grade-level teams, 64–65
  implementing new practices, 61–62
  instructional coaching, 57–58
  instructional resources, 59–60
  staff professional development, 56–57
  stages of concern, 62–63, 62f
  student assessment and outcomes, 58–59
  tasks, 63–64
Educational rejuvenation, 117
Education system, traditional practices, 15–17
End-of-course products, 44
Engagement, communities, 28–29, 30–31, 83–84
Equality vs. equity, 91–92
Equity vs. equality, 91–92
Ethnicity. *See* Race and ethnicity
Every Student Succeeds Act (ESSA), 1
Explicit knowledge, 13
External authorities, 109–110
External regulations, 2–3, 104–106

Faculty members, implementing new practices, 61
Fahey, K., 15, 61, 62, 76, 86
Fairness of outcomes, 91–92
Families, schools and, 14
Fine, S., 4, 116
Formal authority, 79. *See also* Moral authority

Fragmented education system, 24
Freedom in democracy, 6
Fullan, M., 14

Gasoi, E., 61, 65
Gates, B., 2
Gender, 72
Glass, T. E., 72
Glazer, J. L., 33
Glickman, C., 15, 17, 21, 62, 116
Goal of American schools, 4–6
Goals, 4–6, 14–15
Goleman, D., 13
Gordon, S. P., 17, 62
Governance
  democratic structures, 33–34
  direct participation, 34–35, 35f
  focus on, 38
  ideal vs. reality, 32–33
  representational democracy, 34–35, 35f
  rules for, 29–31
  students representation, 32
  type, 33–34
Grade-level teams. *See* Departmental and grade-level teams
Grammatikopoulos, V., 33
Grant funding, 93
Gruenert, S., 14
Guajardo, F., 21
Guajardo, M. A., 21
Guiding rules of decisionmaking, 25–26

Hanauer, N., 2
Hargreaves, A., 13
Hechinger Report, 115
Hensley, F., 15, 61, 62, 76, 86
Hess, F. M., 2, 59
Higher-functioning schools, 39
Hill, N. E., 1
Hutchens, D., 66
Hybrid governance, 34–35, 36f

Ideological conflict, 75
Implementation
  curriculum development and, 54–56
  faculty members and, 61
  new practices, 61–62

Industrial model, 15–16
Inequity, addressing issues of, 74, 90
Information
   gathering, 46–49
   infusing, 46–47
Input-and-selection approach, 67, 68, 68*t*, 69
Instructional budget, 60
Instructional coaches, 28
Instructional coaching, 57–58
Instructional resources, 59–60
Instruction/instructional practices, 12–13
Integration stages of concern, 63
Internal practices of schools, 120
Ippolito, J., 15, 61, 76, 86

Janson, C., 21
Johnson, D. W., 11, 25
Johnson, F. P., 11, 25

Kegan, R., 13
Knight, J., 13
Knowledge
   access to, 47
   gathering information, 46–49
   as power, 47
   prepackaged curriculum, 47

Lahey, L. L., 13
Leadership
   autocratic, 88
   district, 32, 96
Learning
   factors impacting democracy and, 27–29, 28*t*
   principles, 21–22
   professional, 47–48, 48*t*
   restricted thinking about, 16–17
Levinson, M., 117
Local accountability measures, 90
Local reforms, 118
Locus of control, 26–27
Loewus, L., 72
Lunsford, B., 15

Mann, H., 116
McDonald, J. P., 46
McKee, A., 13
McShane, M. Q., 2, 59
Mehta, J., 4, 116
Meier, D., 61, 65
Memorandums of understanding (MOUs), 91
Messages about classes, 76–77
Mette, I. M., 17
Meyer, H. D., 33
Militello, M., 21
Mission of districts. *See* Vision and mission of districts
Money
   instructional resources/budget, 59–60
   officials and administrators, 60
   seed, 92–93
Moral authority, 79–80.
   See also Formal authority
Morgan, G., 67
Multimedia resources, 78
Mutual professional respect, 19

Neo-conventional schools, 18, 18*t*
   dysfunctional behavior, 112–113
No Child Left Behind (NCLB), 1

O'Connor, Sandra Day, 1
Organizational analysis, 75
Organizational vulnerability, 86
Orientation stages of concern, 62–63
Outcomes, student learning, 58–59

Peakview School, decisionmaking at, 129–130
Peck, C., 16
Peer feedback systems, 28
Personal conflict, 75
Pledge, 24–25, 90, 117
   decisionmaking. *See* Decisionmaking
   sample, 123–128
Policies, 117
   external regulations, 104–106
   re-democratizing, 88
   restructuring, 118
Policymakers, 16
Political realities, 32–33
Power, 72
Practical research, valuation of, 90

Index

Practitioner-friendly research, 90
Prepackaged curriculum, 4, 16, 36, 47, 49, 55, 75
Prepackaged evaluation systems, 17
Principal, 85, 115
   ability to mobilize, 82–83
   educational operations and, 31
   as faculty member, 31
Problem-solving process, 40–49, 90, 117
   caveats to, 45
   gathering information, 46–49
   infusing information, 46–47
   internal accountability system, 46
Professional dialogue. *See* Dialogue and conversations
Professional learning, 47–48, 48*t*
Professional organizations, 47
Proficiency-based instruction, 44
Progressing toward agreed-upon district goals, 90
Progressive data source, 43–44, 43*t*
Project-based learning, 44, 77–78
Promise, 19–21, 90, 117
Psychological hardiness, 116
Public–private partnerships, 92
Public sentiments toward schools, 2–3

Race and ethnicity, 72
Race to the Top (RTTT), 16
Ratification process, 34
Refinement stages of concern, 63
Reflective action, 113
Regulations
   external, 104–106
   guidance, 105
Reitzug, U. C., 16
Renewal of schools
   change process, 66–69
   community engagement opportunities, 83–84
   continuum of, 86–87
   creative use of staffing, 78–79
   critical moments, 85–86
   developmental needs, 69–71
   dilemmas, 103–114
   district and, 88–100
   diversification vs. competition, 80–82

educational change, 110–112
educational priorities, 53–65
   framework, 54*f*
   as an internal process, 47
   moral authority, 79–80
   multimedia resources, 78
   opportunities, 84–86
   schedule/scheduling, 79
   as self-driven process, 53
   technology use, 78
Representational democracy, 34, 35*f*
The Republic (Plato), 66
Resource
   allocation, 92
   instructional, 59–60
   multimedia, 78
   use of, 60
Respect, 19
Responsibilities of district, 98
Restorative practices, 44
Restricted thinking about learning, 16–17
Revere High School, 115
Riegel, L., 17
Rosen, J., 115
Ross-Gordon, J. M., 17, 62
Rules for governance, 29–31

The Saber Tooth Curriculum (Benjamin), 40
Santoro, D. A., 30
Schedule/scheduling, 79
Schein, E. H., 17
Schön, D. A., 110
School(s)
   business management approaches to, 16
   as closed systems, 69–70
   control, 97
   coordination, 108–109
   culture. *See* Culture
   dealing with societal issues, 2
   empowering, 89–91
   external control and, 2–3
   goals, 4–6, 14–15
   making difference in community, 73–74
   needs of local communities, 1, 2

School(s) (*continued*)
  problems, 3–4
  public sentiments toward, 2–3
  recapturing essence of, 1–7
  re-democratizing, 88
  restricted views and beliefs, 16–17
  subgroups, 64
  as successful organizations, 12–15
  top-down feedback, 17
  traditional practices, 15–17
  types of, 18–19, 18*t*
School boards, district personnel and, 88–89
School–community partnerships, 98–99
School Improvement Grants (SIGs), 16
School meetings, 19
Seed money, 92–93
Self-governance, 98
Sensitivity for differentiated needs, 90
Shields, C. M., 14
Social satisfaction, 19
Sociocultural differences, 71–73
  control and power, 72
  demographics, 73
  gender, 72
  race and ethnicity, 72
Staff professional development, 56–57
Stages of concern, 62–63, 62*f*
  integration, 63
  orientation, 62–63
  refinement, 63
Standardization, 4
Stiggins, R. J., 90
Student achievement, 2, 11
Student assessment and outcomes, 58–59

Student-centered learning, 115
Subgroups, 65
Successful organizations, 12–15
Summer vacation, 79

Tasks, educational, 63–64
Teachers. *See also* School(s)
  decisions and, 30
  voice and representation, 106–108
Technology, 78. *See also* Multimedia resources
Third-party vendors, 16
Thompson, K., 21
Three-dimensional framework, 117
Top-down feedback, 17
Tough, P., 120

Useem, J., 116

Value, 16–17
  classes, 76–77
  practical research, 90
Veto power, 33–34
Vision and mission of districts, 96–97
Voice, 49, 106–108
Vulnerability. *See* Organizational vulnerability

Walsh, D., 2
Walton, A., 2
Whitaker, T., 14
Wood, G., 116

You, S., 18

Zdenek, R. O., 2

About the Authors

Carl D. Glickman is professor emeritus of education at the University of Georgia (UGA). His career began as a Teacher Corps intern in the rural South, and later he was a principal of award-winning schools in New Hampshire. His university years started at The Ohio State University. He joined the faculty of UGA in 1979 where he founded the Georgia League of Professional Schools, a nationally validated network of K–12 schools devoted to democratic learning of all students. He received the highest faculty career award of the University of Georgia for bringing "stature and distinction" to its mission, and was chosen by students as the faculty member who had "most contributed to their lives, inside and outside the classroom."

Carl served on the boards of the National Campaign for the *Civic Mission of Schools*, Kids Voting U.S.A., the National Commission for Service-Learning, the Foxfire Fund, and the Forum for Education and Democracy. He has been a consultant to state governors and U.S. presidential candidates and is the author of 14 books on school leadership, educational renewal, and the moral imperative of education, two chosen as outstanding books of the year by *Choice Magazine*. In addition, his creative writing stories have won awards, including best memoir of the year by the Southeast Writer's Association. Carl and his spouse, Sara, a former public school teacher, reside in Athens, Georgia, and spend summers with their children and grandchildren in Saint Albans Bay, Vermont.

Ian M. Mette is an associate professor in the Educational Leadership program at the University of Maine. He received his bachelor of science (2003) from the University of New Hampshire and his PhD (2012) from the University of Missouri. He has served as a teacher and central office coordinator, program coordinator for Educational Leadership in the College of Education and Human Development, and is founding editor of the *Journal of Educational Supervision*. In collaboration with multiple school districts, he has established various university–school partnerships that focus on developing leadership pipelines based on individualized professional development needs. Additionally, he regularly coauthor technical reports that are presented to the Education and Cultural Affairs Committee of the Maine State Legislature regarding issues of teacher supervision and evaluation.

Ian lives in Bangor, Maine, with his partner, Dr. Rebecca Schwartz Mette, a clinical psychology faculty member at the University of Maine. They have three wonderful young children, Ellie, Jack, and Gracie, who keep them on their toes in their personal lives. The Mettes enjoy all outdoor activities, including but not limited to camping, hiking, skiing, snowshoeing, and ice fishing. Their Manitou and Somerset friends keep them busy in the summertime, where they are able to reconnect with camp friends that span over 2 decades.